So-Called Experts:

How American Consultants Remade

the Canadian Civil Service, 1918–21

Alasdair Robert

Monographs on Canadian Public Administration – No. 18
Monographies sur l'administration publique canadienne – No. 18

L'Institut d'administration publique du Canada
The Institute of Public Administration of Canada

Canadian Cataloguing in Publication Data

Roberts, Alasdair Scott
  So-called experts

  (Monographs on Canadian public administration
  Monographies sur l'administration publique
  canadienne ; 18)
  ISBN 0-920715-38-9

  1. Civil service reform – Canada – History – 20th century.
  2. Government consultants – United States – History –
  20th century.   I. Institute of Public Administration of
  Canada.   II. Title.   III. Series: Monographs on Canadian
  public administration ; 18.

  JL108.R62 1996   354.71'006   C96-930564-8

PUBLISHED BY / PUBLIÉ PAR

L'INSTITUT D'ADMINISTRATION PUBLIQUE DU CANADA
THE INSTITUTE OF PUBLIC ADMINISTRATION OF CANADA
150 est, av. Eglinton Avenue East, Suite 305
Toronto, Ontario M4P 1E8
Tel: (416) 932-3666
Fax/Télécopieur: (416) 932-3667

Table of Contents

MONOGRAPHS ON CANADIAN PUBLIC ADMINISTRATION

MONOGRAPHIES SUR L'ADMINISTRATION PUBLIQUE CANADIENNE

Iain Gow, Paul Pross
Co-directeurs / Co-editors

This monograph series is sponsored by the Institute of Public Administration of Canada as part of its continuing endeavour to stimulate and publish writing in the field of Canadian public administration. It is intended to be a complement to other publications sponsored by the Institute such as the Canadian Public Administration Series, the magazine *Public Sector Management*, the journal *Canadian Public Administration* and the Case Program in Canadian Public Administration, as well as the proceedings of its public policy seminars. By launching the monograph series for medium-length manuscripts and those of a more specialized nature, the Institute ensures that there is a wide variety of publication formats for authors in public administration. While the first titles were in the area of urban local government, the series is intended to cover the broad public administration field and is under the guidance of the co-editors and of the Research Committee of the Institute.

Cette collection de monographies est parrainée par l'Institut d'administration publique du Canada et témoigne de l'effort suivi de l'Institut pour promouvoir et publier des écrits dans le domaine de l'administration publique canadienne. Elle a été conçue comme un complément aux autres publications parrainées par l'Institut telles la Collection administration publique canadienne, le magazine *Management et secteur public*, la revue *Administration publique du Canada* et le Programme de cas en administration publique canadienne, de même que les comptes rendus de ses colloques sur des questions de politique publique. En lançant la collection de monographies pour les ouvrages de longueur moyenne et ceux de nature plus spécialisée, l'Institut s'assure que les auteurs dans le domaine de l'administration publique disposent d'une grande diversité de formats de publications. Bien que les premiers titres traitaient du gouvernement local urbain, la collection s'étend à l'ensemble du domaine de l'administration publique et est sous la direction des co-directeurs de même que du Comité de recherche de l'Institut.

L'Institut d'administration publique du Canada
The Institute of Public Administration of Canada

Acknowledgements

While writing this paper I have had the benefit of comments from many readers. I would like to express my particular thanks to professors Ted Hodgetts, Iain Gow and Paul Pross for their support of this project, as well as to the members of my thesis committee at the Kennedy School of Government: professors Michael Barzelay, Steven Kelman and Robert Putnam. Don Lenihan provided useful advice, and Chantal Carstens did a wonderful job of proofreading the final draft. I would also like to thank the many archivists, particularly at the National Archives of Canada, who helped me root out the material for this study.

[We cannot] reasonably expect politically appointed department heads, under present conditions in political life, to be in position to know and apply those nice details of business management which mark the difference between efficiency and economy on the one hand and inefficiency and waste on the other. Some political executives are frankly opposed to economy and believe in lavish expenditures; some are not informed about their own departments or feel the task of promoting efficiency hopeless. ... [T]he business management of government ... should be dealt with scientifically by a single authority.

Robert Catherwood, president,
Chicago Civil Service Reform Association, 1910

What firm in Chicago would know about the working out of the Civil Service system of Canada?

A member of Parliament, 1919

1

The "Vicious System" and How We Got It

In 1918–19 the Canadian government adopted two laws that radically changed the character of the federal public service.[1] The laws had been adopted to satisfy Prime Minister Robert Borden's promise to abolish patronage appointments in the whole of the public service. The reforms gave the Civil Service Commission the power to establish organizational plans for other government departments; to classify positions and set salaries; to control appointments, promotions, transfers and dismissals; and to conduct investigations into the efficiency with which government business was being conducted.

This early attempt at "reinventing government" seemed, at first, to be an unalloyed success. An expert at Washington's Brookings Institution who had participated in the design of the reforms boasted that it was the largest single effort at reform ever undertaken by any government in the English-speaking world. Reformers across the U.S., including the leadership of the U.S. National Civil Service Reform League, heralded the project as a demonstration of state-of-the-art progressive government. It quickly led to the undertaking of similar reform projects by the cities of Baltimore and Philadelphia, the states of Georgia, Kentucky, Maryland and South Carolina, and the U.S. government itself. The young man from Chicago who had led the project, Edwin O. Griffenhagen, would later become established as one of the United States' most highly regarded consultants in the field of public administration. His staff comprised many others who would go on to become leaders in the field, including one key assistant who would shortly be appointed secretary of the Civil Service Commission of the State of New Jersey.

Within the federal government, reaction to the new legislation was more tepid: senior officials soon complained that the laws had created an intolerable administrative burden. "I regard the whole system upon which the Commission rests as fundamentally wrong," said Sir Joseph Pope, the under-secretary of state for External Affairs, "The present inflexible, rigid, mechanical, iron-bound system destroys initiative, kills individual effort, [and] is subversive of discipline. ... The classification [is] a positive hindrance to effective administration."[2] Adam Shortt, a recently retired member of the Civil Service Commission and also a highly regarded proponent of reform, wrote that the public service had been put under "a vicious system, detrimental alike to efficiency and merit. The C.S. Commission itself has become a glaring example of a very complex and cumbersome machine frightfully expensive to maintain, creaking with weight and friction, and absorbing much of its energy in its own operation while making endless unnecessary work for the various Departments."[3]

While there have been significant changes to the structure of the public service over the decades, the broad design of the regulatory regime established by the 1918–19 laws persisted and so too did complaints about the burden this regime has imposed on line managers.[4] In 1930, the Royal Commission on Technical and Professional Services (Beatty Commission) concluded that the classification system was "unnecessarily cumbrous," and that the rules governing promotion within the service were "mechanical and lifeless ... [and] needlessly complex."[5] The 1946 Royal Commission on Administrative Classifications in the Public Service (Gordon Commission) concurred:

> Certain of the fundamental difficulties and weaknesses of the civil service today are due to the persistent attempt to work within the confines of this rigid and complex system of classification. ... [It] has hindered the adequate development and utilization of high grade personnel. It has rendered difficult the transfer of individuals not only between departments but within departments. ... It has slowed down and rendered cumbersome the machinery of promotion. ... [T]he complexity of the system entails a large amount of detailed administrative

and paper work and consequently delay, with the result that important positions not infrequently remain vacant for prolonged periods.[6]

The 1961 Royal Commission on Government Organization (Glassco Commission) observed that "the general system of control remains substantially undiminished" and that, while it might ensure the "avoidance of sin," it was also "costly, frustrating, and unproductive."[7] The 1979 Royal Commission on Financial Management and Accountability (Lambert Commission) also urged that deputy heads of departments be given "greater freedom and flexibility to manage" their human resources.[8]

In 1990, the report of the Public Service 2000 project again called for more extensive delegation of those responsibilities to line managers; the project's task force on staffing complained that the "management philosophy" underlying the current personnel management system is one "that favours the exercise of external control rather than the exercise of individual responsibility, a philosophy that favours error prevention rather than accountability, a philosophy that relies on rules rather than judgement."[9] The government introduced a bill, the proposed Public Service Reform Act, in June 1991, to loosen central controls over line managers.[10] John Edwards, a public servant who played a key role in designing the new legislation, characterized it as an attempt to remedy the effects of the 1918–19 reforms:

[M]uch of the debate over ... Bill C-26 has its origin in ... different visions of organizational design and behaviour. The first is the vision of the scientific management school that was so influential in the early part of the century. The vestiges of this school still remain with us to this day. Back then, the experts of Arthur Young and Company [the firm that employed Edwin Griffenhagen] came to Canada from the United States to help set up a professional public service. They held to the firm conviction that for any organization with a given mission there was a best structure, that every job should be carefully defined, and that for every job there was a best person to be found and people should remain in those jobs as long as they wanted and could maintain a level of competence.

It was a mechanistic view of the world of work, of clear-cut and precise specialization of labour, one that assumed considerable organizational stability – so much stability that each step in the process of classifying and filling jobs should be done thoroughly even if it took many months, because each appointment was expected to last for years and years. This resulted in heavy, time-consuming processes and not a great deal of concern for human resource management. Employees were, in essence, seen as cogs in a large machine.

Much of the last 30 years has been, in my view, a battleground between this rigid vision and the realities of the changing environment we face. Today it is difficult to underestimate the ferment and turmoil occurring in most large organizations; skills becoming obsolete, jobs disappearing, the jobs that remain undergoing radical change in content, new approaches to management, quite extraordinary technological impacts, movement toward multi-skilling, with increasing disappearance of barriers to the employment of women and other groups and growing interdependence among functions such as personnel, finance, EDP, communications, and so forth.

In the light of these trends, most people agree that the old vision is now largely unworkable for any organization. The evidence with respect to the public service is there for all to see. There is an elaborate classification system with benchmarks we cannot keep current because of changing technology. In a public service of a little over 200,000 people, there are 100,000 to 150,000 classification actions a year. There is a staffing regime strained to impossible limits, where it takes 90 days or more to conduct a routine competition. ... There are mechanistic systems that prevent good people management, undermine planning and efforts to assist employees – both high and low performers – to develop their potential or to accommodate their personal circumstances.[11]

Given the persistence and importance of the complaints made against the system adopted in 1918–19, one might reasonably ask: why was it adopted in the first place? One common approach to this question begins with the assumption that there are, as the Lambert Commission suggested, "sound historical reasons" for the design of the system.[12] Thus if the system is found to be highly restrictive, it must be, as Taylor Cole once said, that such restrictions were necessary as "a check against the spoilsmen."[13] The administrative burden created by the system, the Glassco Commission suggested, "went unnoticed – or at least, unlamented."[14] The historical model implicit in this approach is one of government as a single decision maker, carefully weighing the benefits and costs of reforms, and consciously designing the civil service regime in order to accommodate purely domestic social forces. As the Public Service 2000 project recently said: "The Public Service is ... uniquely Canadian. It has evolved to reflect our society and culture."[15]

This view of the reforms – which says, in brief, that there must have been something in the character of the federal service in 1918 that demanded that such severe controls be given to the Civil Service Commission – is widespread. It was certainly the view taken by critics of Bill C-26 who argued in 1991 that controls were still needed to control not only political patronage but also "bureaucratic" patronage within the service. "We all know the history of the Public Service," said Margaret Catterall, one of the Liberal opposition's main critics of the bill, "For probably its first fifty-five years, it was not a happy history in terms of patronage, administrative and political":

> Since 1919 it has been the proud claim of Canadians that we have a Public Service where you get a job because you are the best qualified person for that job. This is the merit principle. The Civil Service Commission was established in 1919 specifically to get rid of rampant patronage and favouritism in the Public Service at both the political and the administrative levels. ... Yet here we have again an abandonment of the merit principle, a bill that now says being the best qualified does not count anymore. Your boss, your foreman, your manager, your deputy minister will be able to decide on his or her own if you are good enough to get moved around where the opportunities are to advance and improve your skills. No review and no recourse, totally arbitrary decisions by individuals within the Public Service, and no protection.[16]

Marvin Gandall, a representative of the Economists', Sociologists' and Statisticians' Association, framed the history of the service in much the same way:

Right back to the time of the First World War, Parliament intervened to ensure administrative and political patronage would be curbed in the Public Service. They set up the Public Service Commission at that time. ... What the senior bureaucracy is doing through this bill in effect is attempting to carve out a much greater degree of autonomy for itself. It's doing this in two ways. First, it is saying that it does not have to be bound by the merit principle, which was introduced by Parliament back in 1918 or 1919. Secondly, it is seriously weakening Parliament's chosen instrument, the Public Service Commission, as a regulatory body to ensure the senior bureaucracy respects the merit principle.[17]

Several other Opposition MPs also emphasized the importance of the controls imposed by the 1918–19 reforms as a check against patronage and particularly against bureaucratic patronage, a problem that one member of Parliament argued was "even more insidious" than political patronage,[18] and which several argued was "rampant" before 1919.[19] Another MP asserted that the Civil Service Commission "was established in 1919 ... to prevent management abuse and ensure fair treatment to employees."[20]

There were at least two significant errors in the comments made by critics of Bill C-26. The first lay in the often-repeated assertions that there was no significant effort at civil service reform in the federal service before 1919, that there was no Civil Service Commission before 1919 or that there was no Civil Service Act before 1919.[21] The second lay in the assertion that the reforms had been motivated in large part by "rampant" bureaucratic patronage. These assertions are essential to the conventional narrative about the 1918–19 reforms: they help us make sense of the 1918–19 reforms by suggesting that they were necessary as remedies to the anarchy that prevailed in the federal service before 1919.

The difficulty, however, is that neither of these assertions is supported by the historical record. It is almost certain that what we would now call "bureaucratic patronage" could be found in the federal service in 1917, but it is not the case that this sort of patronage was widely regarded as a problem or that worries about rampant bureaucratic patronage motivated the 1918–19 reforms. The reforms were almost entirely an attempt to remedy the problem of political patronage, which was widely regarded as a moral outrage threatening to undermine the Liberal–Conservative coalition, which had won the election of December 1917. Far from being distrusted, many permanent officials in the federal service were acknowledged as supporters of civil service reform. In fact, it had been deputy minister of finance John Courtney who had pushed the Laurier government to adopt the first rigorous Civil Service Act in 1908. The 1908 act established the Civil Service Commission and set up a system for regulating the "inside service" – the roughly three thousand employees working in Ottawa – which depended heavily on the cooperation of the deputy ministers. Several reliable observers, including the civil service commissioners, believed that this decentralized approach was effective in promoting the merit principle in the inside service.

Another common mistake in the conventional understanding of the 1918–19 reforms was the assumption that the administrative burdens imposed by the reforms were accepted at the time as the price that had to be paid for the introduction of the merit principle. This, as I have intimated earlier and hope to demonstrate in more detail later, was very clearly not the case. The 1918–19 reforms prompted an intense struggle in Ottawa that lasted for five years. Outside observers saw the public side of this fight, which consisted of attempts by some disgruntled backbench members of Parliament to restore patronage within the federal service. But perhaps the most interesting part of the fight was largely private: the struggle of deputies to persuade the commission that administrative costs, which it had imposed on them, were unnecessarily high. It may be, of course, that the deputies' complaints were only rationalizations for their attempts to restore patronage: in fact, some of the Civil Service Commission's staff argued as much. But this requires us to believe that deputies who had been regarded as trustworthy in 1917 had suddenly been corrupted by 1920. It also requires us to discount the testimony of a recently retired commissioner, Adam Shortt, who was widely regarded as a vigorous proponent of the merit principle and who thought that the deputies' complaints were entirely well-grounded.

All of this is to suggest that conventional accounts of the 1918–19 reforms, which assume that there are "sound historical reasons" for the shape of the reforms and the burdens they imposed on line officials, are generally mistaken. Anarchy did not prevail in the federal service and in the inside service, in particular, before 1918. Significant progress towards the establishment of the merit principle had been made, many deputies had cooperated in the implementation of a decentralized merit system, and many of these same deputies had vigorously objected to the much more highly centralized merit system in 1918–19. The shape of the 1918–19 reforms cannot be properly understood solely as a product of the political and administrative conditions that existed in Ottawa at the time of the reforms.

Contemporary interpretations of the reform effort – those which fall in the "sound historical reasons" school – differ significantly from those made by academic observers at the time of the reforms. These earlier commentators were much less inclined to suppose that there were good reasons for the adoption of the new system. The picture these early commentators paint, instead, is one in which the constituents of the Canadian political community argue fiercely about the wisdom of the proposed reforms, in which possibilities for less restrictive but equally effective merit reforms are overlooked, and in which a tired and distracted political executive is finally gulled by American consultants of doubtful competence.

In fact, the role of these consultants – a staff of twenty-seven men employed by Arthur Young and Company of Chicago and led by Edwin O. Griffenhagen – is given great emphasis in early accounts of the attempt at civil service reform. In 1923, Adam Shortt wrote a confidential letter to his friend and fellow reformer William Grant, principal of Upper Canada College, who was then attempting to establish an organization like the U.S. National Civil Service Reform League and who was looking for speakers on public service reform:

> You may understand ... how difficult it would be for either A.K. Maclean or Sir George Foster, or even Mr. Rowell [all ministers who had guided the reforms through Parliament] to speak freely or serviceably on the subject of C.S. Reform when they were the innocent but misguided victims of the American Experts who so completely gained the ears of the ministers and virtually usurped for a time the functions of the Civil Service Commission and particularly of Dr. Roche [one of the commissioners]; for whom I have the greatest personal respect, and, I must add, commiseration. ... There are some

good Americans such as Ex President Eliot of Harvard, who have not been deceived by the clotted verbiage in which dis-organization is named *re-organization* and petrified anarchy called *classification*. Now, however, all Americans are suspect.[22]

William Grant later picked up this theme himself, presenting the 1918–23 reforms as

a very difficult job, requiring a mixture of expertise and common sense. Unfortunately, Sir Robert Borden, overworked and weary, turned the matter over to the Commission. Still more unfortunately the Commission ... selected an American firm of supposed experts. ... Had we had a Standing Committee of the House, to which their report could have been referred, the harm might have been undone. But we had no such Standing Committee. The report was indeed discussed in the House of Commons; but the voice of wisdom was lost in clamour about individual cases. The root principles of administration were lost sight of.[23]

Robert Macgregor Dawson, the author of the first general work on the Canadian civil service, adopted the same interpretation of events:

In a very weak moment a company of American experts was imported to conduct the work, the government apparently having some inside information on civil service efficiency in the United States which has not yet been disclosed to a somewhat skeptical world. The experts arrived, laboured for months ... and then returned to Chicago, leaving behind them proposals which completely transformed the general scheme of civil service organization as it existed at that time. These proposals were accepted in due course by a credulous Parliament with scarcely a word of protest and with no realization of the revolutionary changes which the Act involved.[24]

Many participants in the debate over the 1918–19 reforms shared this scepticism about the so-called "experts": I will later show that challenges to the authority of Griffenhagen and his staff, and to a lesser degree to the authority of staff within the Civil Service Commission, were a major theme in arguments about the reforms. One civil service leader even called Griffenhagen an "imposter and charlatan ... with [a name] reminiscent of his Majesty's late enemies."[25]

A second approach to explaining the 1918–19 reforms consists, therefore, of an exercise in demonology in which fault for the costs imposed upon the Canadian public service in those years is laid on the shoulders of Edwin O. Griffenhagen. This approach comes a little nearer to the truth of what happened in 1918–19 but still has a substantial defect. The error is to focus on Edwin Griffenhagen alone, or on Edwin Griffenhagen and his staff, and to miss the much broader story about the character of the U.S. civil service reform movement in the early years of this century.

Griffenhagen was one member of a very young "expert community," a group of like-minded individuals who were not only interested in civil service reform but who purported to be experts on the subject. These individuals – some community leaders and some members of the staff of the many American civil service commissions – communicated regularly with one another through organizations such as the U.S. National Civil Service Reform League, the U.S. National Municipal League and particularly the U.S. National Assembly of Civil Service Commissions, which had been established in 1906. They were almost exclusively American and predominantly engaged in municipal reform, and their understanding of the character of the reform problem was heavily influenced by their view of the political and administrative conditions confronting American cities at the turn of the century. The worldview of this expert community was particularly influenced by the experience of reformers from Chicago, whose city government was chaotic and systematically corrupt.

This community had put forward a claim to authority on the subject of civil service reform, but that is not to say that this claim was readily accepted by other participants in debates over the reform of state and local governments. On the contrary, the members of this community often found, as Griffenhagen found in Ottawa, that their claim to expertise was regarded dimly, and that, as a consequence, the prospects for the adoption of their proposed reforms were also dim. As a consequence, these reformers had, by 1917, developed standardized ways of arguing about their right to speak authoritatively on the subject of reform. Later I will characterize the bundle of arguments that were typically used for this purpose as a *rhetorical strategy*. One argument in this strategy was that civil service reform – or public personnel administration, as the field would shortly come to be known – was a "science" that could only be properly discussed by trained technicians. A second argument consisted of an attack on the motives of individuals who challenged the authority of the experts. A third argument consisted of a demonstration that the members of the expert community had reached agreement that certain reforms should be regarded as "best practice."

Griffenhagen imported this rhetorical strategy into Canada and relied on it heavily in the debate over reform in the years 1918–23. The staff of the newly expanded Canadian Civil Service Commission – who had also become members of the community of experts on civil service reform – also relied on the same modes of argument. Much of the experts' unfortunate behaviour in these years, including, their dogmatism and unwillingness to accommodate criticisms of their reforms, can be described as effects of this rhetorical strategy. The experts in Ottawa clung to this strategy as the only means of substantiating their authority as experts on civil service reform; more broadly, however, they clung to it because it was the means chosen by the expert community as a whole to be used to defend themselves in dozens of arguments about civil service reform in states and municipalities across the United States.

Readers will find that to a large degree the story of the Canadian reforms is not a story about Canada at all. It is, instead, largely a story about the problems of the U.S. civil service reform movement, which paradoxically came to regard the Canadian reforms as a model of the kind of reforms it hoped would be adopted by U.S. governments as the remedy for their particular political and administrative problems. This is a fact that has never been recognized in Canadian commentaries on the 1918–19 reforms.

As the debate over Bill C-26 suggested, our judgments about contemporary reforms are still coloured by our understanding of what happened in 1918–19, and for this reason alone it is important to get our history of those reforms right. There is, however, also a larger purpose to be served by this study. It began as part of a doctoral thesis that was intended to shed light on the relationship between people who claim to be experts in the subject of management and the people who look to these experts for advice. The thesis had two objectives: first, to understand why experts sometimes provide bad advice to their clients; and second, to understand how certain ideas come to be established as "conventional wisdom" within expert communities.

My answers to these questions are laid out in detail in the thesis itself,[26] but readers may be interested in a brief summary of the main line of argument. I begin with the proposition that the right of expert communities to wield authority over problems in a certain domain is constantly under attack, and that one of the major tasks that must be undertaken by any expert community is the rhetorical task of inventing and disseminating arguments that show why the community's claim to authority is a reasonable one. The thesis examines the rhetorical strategies – the bundle of arguments and routines – that have historically been used by expert communities to substantiate their claim to authority over problems in the field of management. The first part, which provides the material for this study, examines the rhetorical problems of the civil service reform movement between 1907 and 1922; the second examines those of the public administration community between 1927 and 1937, focusing particularly on the work of the Brownlow Committee in 1936–37[27]; and the third examines those of the contemporary public management community.[28] I argue that the rhetorical strategies employed by these expert communities imposed significant constraints on the behaviour of individuals within them, sometimes causing them to provide bad advice to clients outside the expert community. I briefly explore some of the practical implications of this line of analysis in the final chapter of this monograph.

A major task for any expert community consists in deciding what counts as reliable knowledge in a certain field. In other words, expert communities are engaged in the epistemological project of deciding what we know about certain problems and what we ought to do about them. There is a widespread popular notion that this project is one that is undertaken far away from the bustle of daily life in an "objective" or "independent" way. I argue that this is very often anything but the case. The epistemological project ("What do we know about subject X? What should we advise about problem Y?") is invariably tied up with the project of crafting an effective rhetorical strategy ("How do we get people to trust us?"). The evolution of ideas in a certain field is conditioned by the broader struggle of the expert community to substantiate its claim to authority in terms that are persuasive to other important social actors. The story of the 1918–19 reforms will, incidentally, provide an illustration of this general point.

This study is part of a growing literature that takes a rhetorical approach to problems of management and bureaucratic reform.[29] By this, I mean that it pays particular attention to the kinds of arguments used by different actors within public organizations, attempts to understand why some arguments are preferred over others and assesses the consequences of relying on one argument over another. This literature has evolved in reaction to earlier works that have tended, sometimes unconsciously, to frame the internal life of organizations as though they were games or processes of "power politics" very narrowly defined. More recently, scholars have recognized that the internal life of organizations is richer than the game-based approach would suggest. While individuals within organizations certainly do rely on the crude exercise of power, they also appeal to each other through arguments, and they have clear ideas about what a reasonable argument entails. The rhetorical approach studies these appeals and attempts, among other things, to understand why we argue the way we do.

2

Burglar-Proofing the Chicago Civil Service

The system adopted in Canada in 1918–19 was known among American civil service reformers as the "Chicago Idea" or the "Chicago Plan." It was developed by Chicagoan reformers between 1907 and 1915, and its design can be best understood as a response to the social and political conditions that confronted those reformers at that time. If there are "sound historical reasons" for the shape of the reforms adopted in Canada in 1918–19, they must be found in Chicago.

At the turn of the century, the city of Chicago was struggling to manage a phenomenal rate of growth. The population of Chicago tripled to 1.5 million people in the twenty years before 1900, and immigration to the city had not yet abated. Living conditions in some parts of the city were appalling. Housing was crowded and ramshackle; services such as sanitation, police and fire protection, education and street maintenance were completely inadequate. Furthermore, local government seemed incapable of responding effectively to these problems.

Local government in Chicago was confronted with two great challenges at the turn of the century. The first was a fragmentation of authority between a myriad of governments and special-purpose agencies. "The formal government [of Chicago] is chaos," the political scientist (and one-time alderman) Charles Merriam argued.[30] Legislative authority was divided between the Illinois state legislature, the city government, the Cook County Board of Commissioners, three park districts, several neighbouring townships and a number of independent boards. Within the city government, power was highly diffused. Chicago had a governing structure typical of many nineteenth-century American municipalities, with a weak mayor and a strong council. Party unity among the sixty-eight aldermen was marginal. There was no rationalized system of budget-making, and aldermen even set the salaries for individual employees. Budget-making was a free-for-all: aldermen on the city's finance committee "sat around the table for weeks, and sometimes months, taking up each position [in the service] separately, and deciding, often on personal grounds, what salary to recommend. Outside, the corridors would be full of employees and their friends to urge their claims upon members of the committee."[31]

The "chaos" of local government was aggravated by widespread corruption. The city council itself "was the heart of corruption."[32] In the 1890s it had become notorious for the practice of taking bribes in exchange for legislation. ("If you want to get anything out of the council," one businessman said, "the quickest way is to pay for it."[33]) The most corrupt of these aldermen – known as the "grey wolves" – still held considerable power a decade later. Furthermore, the corruption had seeped into the administrative apparatus of the city as well. Many city departments, including the police force, were rife with graft-taking and had close links with organized crime. In 1911, several treasurers of local governments within Cook County were under charges for illegal appropriation of funds.[34]

By the turn of the century, many businessmen and professionals in the Chicago area, frustrated by the city's inability to provide services and offended by pervasive corruption, had begun to campaign actively for reform of the city government. They worked through a network of clubs and associations, such as the City Club, the Civic Federation, the Union League Club, the Citizens' Association, the Municipal Voters' League, the Civil Service Reform Association and others. There were, of course, similar efforts at mobilization in other major cities, and we have come, in retrospect, to refer to this broad mobilization as the Progressive movement.[35]

Richard Hofstadter has argued that the political strategy pursued by Progressive reformers had two distinctive characteristics. The first was a heavy emphasis on the investigation and revelation of corruption within public institutions. In this regard, reformers were influenced by "muckraking" journalists, such as Ida May Tarbell and Lincoln Steffens, and realist novelists, such as Upton

Sinclair whose book *The Jungle,* a loose fictional account of work in Chicago's meat-packing plants, was published in 1906. Hofstadter argues: "The Progressive mind was characteristically a journalistic mind. ... The muckraker was a central figure. Before there could be action, there must be information and exhortation. Grievances had to be given specific objects, and these the muckraker supplied."[36] This faith in the "tonic effect" of publicity was combined with a belief that reform was primarily a problem of making and enforcing legislation; corruption was conceived as a matter of "lawlessness" to be remedied by the imposition of stronger laws.[37]

The reform movement in Chicago shared both of these characteristics. Between 1900 and 1910, the clubs and associations that anchored the movement sponsored a series of inquiries into the city's social and political problems. The Civic Federation investigated meat and milk inspection within city limits and reported on the "scandalous" condition of the judicial system,[38] the City Club sponsored an investigation of corruption in the police department and a study of the misuse of municipal revenues,[39] the Citizens' Association revealed violations of city election laws,[40] the Chicago Women's Club completed an exposé of working conditions for women,[41] and the Municipal Voters' League conducted a continuing inquiry into corrupt practices by the streetcar monopolies.

Allied to this investigatory work were a series of unsuccessful campaigns for more powerful anti-corruption laws. The Chicago Civil Service Reform Association succeeded in persuading the city to adopt a civil service law in 1895, but this had been undermined by the mayor's unwillingness to enforce the law.[42] The Civic Federation moved on to a campaign for primary law reform intended to wrest party nominations away from the control of machine politicians, which was also unsuccessful.[43] Campaigns for adoption of a "corrupt practices act" and for laws to break up the streetcar monopolies also failed.[44] A five-year attempt by reformers to obtain a new charter to reorganize city government was defeated in a municipal referendum in November 1907.[45]

THE CIVIL SERVICE COMMISSION AS AN INSTRUMENT OF REFORM

In 1908, the reform community, frustrated by this succession of failures, chanced upon another path for pursuing reform of the municipal government. In the 1907 municipal election, reformers had succeeded in winning a significant minority of council seats. Furthermore, the new mayor, Fred Busse, if not himself an active reformer, seemed conscious of the growing political power of the reform element.[46] One of his first acts had been to appoint a reformer, Elton Lower, to head the Civil Service Commission that had been established in 1895.

Lower immediately became the subject of a determined lobby by Robert Catherwood, a young patent lawyer who had arrived in Chicago at the height of the scandals over aldermanic corruption and who was now president of Chicago's Civil Service Reform Association.[47] Catherwood wanted Lower to define the responsibilities of the commission much more broadly than they had ever been defined before. He had developed a scheme – what he called an "efficiency plan" – that would not only give the commission the power to screen appointments to the municipal service, but also to monitor the performance of employees while in the service, control the use of personnel and study the organization of work in city departments.[48] Lower was sympathetic to the plan and believed that the drafting of the 1895 act might give statutory authority to adopt it, but he lacked the money with which to hire Catherwood's proposed staff of "efficiency examiners."

Charles Merriam soon provided the money that Catherwood's plan required. Elected to city council in February 1909, Merriam immediately began attacking corruption within the Busse administration and lobbied for a special commission to study municipal expenditures.[49] The special commission was appointed in June 1909 and soon began a sweeping investigation that "disclosed startling conditions of waste, extravagance, and graft in city departments."[50] Catherwood suggested to Merriam that the Civil Service Commission could be the instrument with which the problems Merriam's special commission had uncovered could be remedied. Merriam agreed and recommended that the city council appropriate funds for a new "efficiency division" within the Civil Service Commission that would "concentrate the power of the city government in an effort to increase the efficiency of the public service."[51] In January 1910, the council, embarrassed by the Merriam report, voted to fund the commission's new "efficiency division." The commission quickly hired a small staff for the division.

One of the keenest members of the new staff was a young civil engineer named Edwin Griffenhagen. Later in his career, Griffenhagen would be recognized as one of the leading experts in public administration in North America.[52] In 1910, however, Griffenhagen was very much a newcomer to the field. He was twenty-four years old and had graduated from Chicago's Armour Institute of Technology scarcely four years before. He had worked briefly as a mining engineer in Alaska, as an office engineer for the Chicago–Minneapolis–St. Paul Railway and then briefly as an architectual engineer for the City of Chicago.[53] Griffenhagen was shortly joined in the efficiency division by another young engineer, Louis Jacobs; the two were soon adopted by Catherwood as his protegés.

The efficiency division immediately became the main instrument by which the reform community sought to pursue the goals that had eluded them in the previous decade. Its own work was similar in form to that which reform clubs and associations had undertaken: a heavy emphasis on exposés of corruption and waste in the municipal service, accompanied by increasingly heavy regulation of officials in the line departments.

Between 1910 and 1912, the efficiency division launched inquiries into every aspect of city administration, and "practically every investigation resulted in removal of inefficient or dishonest employees."[54] One series of investigations found "wholesale fraud" in licensing and inspection services.[55] The commission reported:

> An exhaustive investigation was made of the Bureau of Food Inspection. ... The [efficiency] [d]ivision studied the methods of dairy inspection in the country, and milk, stores, depot, meat and other kinds of inspection in the city. ... As a result of the division's report and the testimony of its members before the Commission, the head of the bureau resigned.[56]

Other investigations resulted in the dismissal of the superintendent of sewers and the superintendent of dumps[57]; afterwards the efficiency division designed a new and "scientific" plan for street cleaning and garbage collection.[58] Another investigation exposed "intolerable conditions" in the building department: "fifteen employees were separated from the service, either through resignation under charges or fear of charges, or by discharge after trial. ... It is needless to say that these results ... put the fear of God into those left."[59] Yet another inquiry studied "[the] connection between the Police Department and the various criminal classes in the city of Chicago," focusing particularly on Chicago's First Ward, the home of the city's most notorious machine aldermen.[60] Robert Catherwood described the scope of the investigation:

[The staff of the efficiency division] devoted their attention, first, to gambling; secondly, to violations of the order of the general superintendent of police of April 28, 1910, concerning (1) The entering of boys of under eighteen years of age into disreputable houses; (2) the harboring of inmates under legal age; (3) forcible detention (white slave trade); (4) the presence of women in saloons; (5) indecent attire; (7) street walking and soliciting; (8) signs, lights, colors or devices; (9) obscene exhibitions; (10) houses of ill fame, outside restricted districts; (11) the sale of liquor in houses; (12) the sale of liquor after 1 a.m. It also investigated the trade in cocaine, opium, and other drugs; closed up these places and got evidence not only against the sellers but certain physicians and wholesale drug houses. ...

One hundred fifty of the highest police officials have been discharged. ... The general superintendent of the police is so discredited that his removal by the mayor may be safely predicted. ... The feeling is that the mayor is cordially behind the "shake-up," but, if he is not, the commission is at present so strong, that neither the mayor nor any political force is strong enough to stop the investigation.[61]

Spurred on by these revelations, the Civil Service Commission also set about eliminating, where possible, the discretion of line officials in personnel matters. Robert Catherwood described this aspect of the commission's work as "burglar proofing,"[62] a phrase which fairly represented his view of the character of most line managers. Edwin Griffenhagen developed an increasingly detailed classification system, designed to remove the possibility of favouritism or "logrolling" within the service and to "bring into the light" the fact that the work actually done by civil servants differed from the work they purported to do.[63] The commission asserted its right to control not only appointments to the service, but promotions and dismissals as well, to keep an "absolute check on the work of employees" at every stage of their career.[64] In making promotion decisions, one reformer explained, "the Commission certainly cannot not be biased, nor influenced by the decision of the head of the department. The decision of the head of the department may be due to ulterior motives."[65] In a similar vein, Robert Catherwood argued that the dismissal power could not be delegated to line authorities since it would be "frequently exercised in behalf of outside interests and to forward political ambitions."[66] To guide its promotion and dismissal decisions, Louis Jacobs refined a system for "efficiency rating" of employees – a single quantitative measure of the efficiency of each employee, to be administered by the commission itself. Elton Lower boasted, "We have eliminated from this record ... everything that is a matter of opinion or judgement."[67]

3

The Reformers' Struggle for Credibility

Within two years, the reforms that had been designed in Chicago had also been adopted by other governments in Illinois. In 1910, Robert Catherwood had led a successful statewide referendum campaign on civil service reform, and in the following year, the Illinois general assembly passed laws mandating reform of the civil services of Cook County, the three Chicago park districts and the state government itself.[68] Griffenhagen left Chicago's efficiency division to become superintendent of employment of the South Park Civil Service Commission. Catherwood himself became a member of the Cook County Civil Service Commission where he again supervised the installation of his "efficiency system." Shortly after Catherwood's arrival, the president of the Cook County Commission observed that the statute governing their work "is one of the most far-reaching of all existing civil service laws. ... [I]n my opinion, the commission will be the dominating power in Cook County affairs. ... [I]t is a law that places upon us the duty of supervising every job in the county, and ... the duty almost of supervising the executive and administrative affairs of all these offices."[69]

Despite these advances, the reformers' political foundation was still highly unstable. Charles Merriam assessed the situation on the Chicago council during his tenure as alderman in the following way: "We calculated that one-third of the members were on the market; one-third were not for sale; and one-third were watching the press and the public, with wavering impulses."[70] It was not satisfactory, therefore, for reformers to occupy themselves with the tasks of setting up new commissions and efficiency divisions, making classifications or conducting investigations; they also had to worry about the problem of keeping public opinion – and thus the wavering one-third of council – on their side. "The battle for civic reform," Clifford Patton argues, "... was a struggle for the enlistment of public opinion. ... Crusaders and pressure groups armed themselves with propaganda techniques – of a sort – and set out to arouse a dormant and irresponsible electorate."[71] To engage in this struggle, reformers had to invent a *rhetorical strategy* to accompany their reform proposals – a combination of arguments that seemed likely to persuade politically important segments of the public that the proposals deserved support. In Chicago, this strategy relied on three major themes:

1. *Something old: the attack on motives.* One of the main themes within the reformers' strategy was a legacy from an earlier period of civil service reform that had flourished from the end of the Civil War until shortly after the passage of the federal Pendleton Act in 1883. This theme consisted of an attack on the motives of individuals who criticized reforms. Reformers were presented as defenders of the "public interest," while their opponents were typically presented as individuals who had subordinated the public good to some narrow private interest.[72] One of the major purposes of investigations such as those undertaken by the efficiency division was to illustrate how politicians, department heads and their subordinates had corrupted the system for private gain. Alternative and more flattering interpretations of the motives of the reformers' critics were generally dismissed. The world became one divided into two camps: "venal crooks," on one side, and "saintly paragons," on the other.[73]

2. *Something borrowed: the appeal to science.* It is perhaps not surprising that reformers in Chicago also began couching their prescriptions for reform in the vocabulary of science. In 1910–11, the "scientific management" movement was reaching the crest of its popularity. Louis Brandeis' appeal to the virtues of scientific management during the Interstate Commerce Commission's hearing of the Eastern Rate case in 1910–11 had brought nationwide attention to the movement, as had the congressional hearings on the introduction of scientific management to the Watertown Arsenal in 1911–12. These events were clearly in the minds of the Chicago reformers as they went about crafting their arguments about civil

service reform.[74] It should be noted, however, that the civil service reformers seem to have worked at a distance from the leading proponents of scientific management; men such as Frederick Taylor or Frank Gilbreth never participated in the municipal reform movement. The reformers were merely appropriating ideas that proponents of scientific management had made familiar parts of the popular culture.

The vocabulary of scientific management served important purposes for municipal reformers. First, it gave an air of practicality or hardheadedness to the call for reform. The earlier generation of reformers had often been criticized on precisely this ground. Ari Hoogenboom observes that early reformers were often dismissed by their opponents as "'damned literary fellows' who knew nothing of practical politics."[75] Clifford Patton says of the earlier reform movement:

> There were countless hindrances to its effectiveness. ... To the average ear there was something distasteful about the word "reform." It suggested denunciation, fault-finding, prudishness. Because many professional reformers were incompetent and untrained, the group as a whole came to be looked upon generally as cranks and theorists.[76]

By emphasizing the rhetoric of the scientific management movement, the new generation of reformers could distinguish themselves from their predecessors. (The effect was appreciated by the reformers themselves: "I belong to the class of dreamers," the patrician reformer Richard Henry Dana told his younger colleagues in 1916, "[but] you are practical men."[77]) The "chaos" of municipal government could now be attacked not only as evidence of sinfulness but also on a new, more "practical" ground: that of inefficiency. Furthermore, the use of the vocabulary implied that the reforms being put forward had already been tested, and that they would generate in the public sector the same benefits that "scientific management" had already produced in the private sector.

The appeal to science had a second advantage: it provided a rationale for the transfer of power away from line managers to the staff of the Civil Service Commission. After all, one of the major entailments of the claim that management was a "science" was the proposition that the only persons who should be permitted to exercise managerial authority were those who had been properly trained in that science. The idea that "brain work" could be centralized in a "specially trained planning department" was one of the central premises of the scientific management movement,[78] and this was carried over into the municipal reform movement as a natural complement to the proposition that political executives and line managers were too corrupt to be trusted with much discretion. It provided a rationale for the reformers' attempts to "concentrate the power of city government" within the Civil Service Commission. In 1910, Robert Catherwood argued:

> [We cannot] reasonably expect politically appointed department heads, under present conditions in political life, to be in position to know and apply those nice details of business management which mark the difference between efficiency and economy on the one hand and inefficiency and waste on the other. Some political executives are frankly opposed to economy and believe in lavish expenditures; some are not informed about their own departments or feel the task of promoting efficiency hopeless. ... [T]he business management of government, as distinguished from the politics and management which determines general policies, is best dealt with as a unit – a problem of the whole civil service – and it should be dealt with scientifically by a single authority.[79]

In 1913, Catherwood again argued:

> The problem [of civil service reform] is a technical problem. The experts to deal with it must be educated and trained with care. ... The prompt removal of incompetent employees, the task of getting good men into the service and keeping them there, the improvement of administrative methods, the training of employees for the performance of duty, the correction of organization and defective conditions of employment, the comparison of results with outlay, the preparation of the budget in its employment as distinguished from its financial aspects, the measurement of service and the correlation therewith of pay, and the collection of information concerning the service for the use of responsible executive officers, are all technical problems. ... There is no more reason for calling upon the chief execu-

tive and his department heads to do this work for themselves than
there is for requiring them to design battleships, stoke furnaces or
prescribe medicines for sick paupers.[80]

Catherwood's two protegés, Edwin Griffenhagen and Louis
Jacobs, also subscribed to the view that civil service reform should
be regarded as a "science," and as time progressed their understanding of the subject became thoroughly imbued with the rhetoric of science. In 1924, Griffenhagen prefaced a history of the
Chicago reforms with this observation:

> The reading of the history of a science almost invariably creates a
> feeling of wonder in the student at the difficulties that were encoun-
> tered in arriving at what seem to be the simplest and most obvious
> truths. ... A student of the problems of public personnel administra-
> tion will find this to be his experience as he examines the record of
> progress with regard to those processes most important in the mod-
> ern conception of what such administration should be.[81]

Griffenhagen described the classification system itself as the foundation for the whole field of public personnel administration,
much as classificatory schemes served as the foundation for study
in the "other branches of science":

> The establishment of a common language for the interchange of
> ideas through agreement on a standard terminology has had much to
> do with the acceleration of progress in the physical sciences. An
> appropriate occupational classification provides a similar aid in the
> field of personnel administration. ... [T]he very definition of a "sci-
> ence" must include some reference to the idea of classification, and if
> there is to be any justification for using the word "scientific" in con-
> nection with any plan of personnel administration, it must be predi-
> cated upon a classification of the subject matter.[82]

It followed that there were "scientific principles" governing the
design of the classification, as well as the "investigatorial method"
used by the commission staff in order to collect and sort through
the information required to make and administer the classification.[83]

3. *Something new: the appeal to consensus.* The two major themes that dominated the rhetoric of reform in Chicago during the heyday of the efficiency division – the attack on motives and the appeal to science – were easily available to reformers: one was a legacy from earlier reformers, and the other had been established in popular culture by proponents of scientific management. After 1910, however, Chicago's reformers began the more difficult project of building a third theme: that the Chicago Plan had been endorsed by a much broader community of civil service experts.

Although the Chicago Plan soon became well known to municipal reformers in other cities and even influenced reforms in several cities in the western United States,[84] it was hardly the only plan for municipal reform then in circulation. The national reform movement was then in what the reformer Albert Faught called the "laboratory stage of governmental science":

> In the forum of public opinion today there are being discussed the merits and defects of many important experiments in selecting and removing public officials. ... The nation as a whole recognizes the evils and dangers which accompany the old order of government by political machines maintained by election frauds and chicanery and supported by the spoils system. As to the proper remedies, there is still wide divergence of opinion, and we have not yet obtained a final answer to Tweed's questions as to what we are going to do about it.[85]

Within the national reform community, the Chicago Plan competed with a host of others: the Dallas Idea, the Des Moines Plan, the Dayton Plan, the Berkeley Plan, the Wisconsin Idea, the Ashtabula Plan, "and so on," the head of Chicago's efficiency division complained, "ad infinitum."[86]

For Chicago reformers, attempting to persuade their own community of the value of the Chicago Plan, the proliferation of alternative plans caused serious concern. It undermined the argument that there were definite principles governing reform. It also gave opponents of reform an opportunity to excuse their inaction: they could purport to be confused about the best course of reform rather than be implacably opposed to any reform at all. The case for reform would be strengthened, the Chicago reformers thought, if the "chief Civil Service forces of the country" could be united in their endorsement of only one plan for civil service reform.[87]

There were three national associations through which it was possible for the Chicago reformers to reach the "chief Civil Service forces." The first and oldest was the National Civil Service Reform League, founded in 1881, of which Catherwood's Chicago Civil Service Reform Association was a key member. The others were the National Municipal League, an association of municipal administrators and reformers, begun in 1894, and the National Assembly of Civil Service Commissions, begun in 1906 by representatives of twenty state and local civil service commissions. Chicago reformers began lobbying these three associations to adopt a "model civil service law" as early as 1910. Catherwood, Griffenhagen and Jacobs all joined in this campaign, and by 1913 the three associations had established a joint committee to reach "a definite and concrete answer to the question: 'What are the essential principles of a model civil service law for American states, counties, and cities?'"[88] Catherwood was appointed to the committee and soon became recognized as the "leading spirit" in the development of the new Model Civil Service Law.[89]

The quest for a model law was premised on another entailment of the appeal to science: that all battles for civil service reform were essentially alike and that there could be, therefore, general principles for reform suited to all these cases. In the three years these associations debated over the model law, this premise was never directly challenged. However, there was intense debate about what the principles themselves should be. Much of this debate was provoked by the Illinois reformers who insisted from the start that the Model Civil Service Law should be modelled on the Chicago Plan.

Reformers from other jurisdictions had qualms about the "fearless and original" provisions Catherwood insisted should be put into the model law.[90] One of these was a provision that would have the commissioners themselves chosen by competitive examination. However, other reformers were also disturbed by the amount of power Catherwood's law would remove from line managers and concentrate in the Civil Service Commission. In 1914, a member of the Philadelphia Commission resigned from the drafting committee after distributing a report that said the model law would give civil service commissions too much power over line managers.[91] A

Pueblo civil service commissioner agreed in terms that anticipated the character of the debate that would arise in Ottawa in a few years' time:

> I can think of no greater calamity to the general movement for the adoption of the merit system than the approval of the national assembly of this model law. ... The law is framed upon the assumption that the chief executive will be out of sympathy with the merit system, and that the whole administration will be organized to overthrow it, hence the framers of the model law would tie the hands of the appointing authorities, and take from them much of the responsibility for the efficiency of the service.
>
> In my opinion, we shall never be able to eliminate the spoils system and establish the merit system upon a firm foundation, by transferring responsibility from the officer who is elected or appointed to assume that responsibility to a civil service commission which knows little of the work of the department. ... The success of the merit system in the long run will depend upon the careful and cautious observance of the fundamental right of the appointing authority to have some discretion in the appointment and removal of his subordinates. ... The proposed model law will only tend to foster the spirit of suspicion and antagonism on the part of administrative officials which is in my opinion disastrous to the proper enforcement of any law.[92]

The Illinois delegation refused to yield to the criticisms, insisting that any compromise with the strict provisions of the model law would be sure to promote corruption within the civil service. "[I]f your executive officers are responsible for the merit system," Catherwood asked, obviously thinking of his experience in Chicago, "what right have you got to interfere and annoy and bother them? One of two things are going to happen. Either the merit system, consisting of merit employment as a whole has got to be administered on merit principles, or else you have got to go to the extreme and have a spoils system pure and simple."[93]

The debate over Catherwood's draft of the model law continued throughout the 1914 and 1915 meetings of the national assembly. Catherwood, by now a member of the assembly's executive council, pushed for a vote to endorse his model law; other reformers, however, still balked at its provisions. Consensus proved elusive. Yet, at the same time, members of the assembly felt increasing pressure to make some authoritative statement on civil service reform. The reform movement suffered several setbacks in these years. Political opposition had stalled reform in New York City and in the State of New York,[94] and new administrations in Philadelphia and Cleveland had attempted to weaken their civil service laws.[95] In 1916, campaigns for the repeal of civil service laws were begun in St. Paul and Kalamazoo.[96]

However, the most severe attacks on reform were felt in Illinois. In 1913, a court challenge succeeded in severely restricting the authority of the Cook County Civil Service Commission.[97] In Chicago itself, the situation was worse. In the mayoral election of June 1915, the Progressive candidate had been defeated by William Hale Thompson, an "outrageous personality" who eventually "became famous for his buffoonery, his tolerance for gangsterism, and his general willingness to offend reform sensibilities."[98] Within weeks of his election, Thompson appointed new civil service commissioners – "politicians of the spoils type" – who in turn immediately abolished the commission's efficiency division.[99] "The spoils system swept over the city like a noxious blight," Charles Merriam later wrote, "The city hall became a symbol for corruption and incompetence."[100] One senior city official, attacked by the mayor for resisting patronage appointments, killed himself, leaving a suicide note that appealed to the people of Chicago to protect the administration from "spoils and graft."[101] By the time Catherwood's model law came before the assembly for final consideration in June 1916, the Illinois delegation was fighting a desperate battle against opponents who dismissed them as "phoney reformers."[102] Only a few weeks before the 1916 conference, Catherwood's Civil Service Reform Association had sponsored a protest rally in the Chicago auditorium against the Thompson administration.[103]

The Illinois delegates arrived at the 1916 conference demanding an unequivocal endorsement of the strongest possible model law. However, other members of the assembly were still ambivalent about the severity of Catherwood's draft. Henry Moskowitz, the president of the New York City Commission, expressed his own doubts:

[F]rom a purely theoretical point of view it would not be difficult for me to subscribe to it, but I think there is also a responsibility which rests upon this Assembly consisting of responsible officials to consider whether they can at this time take a position that is abstractly right, theoretically sound, and yet ... will not find, in many cities, the sympathy of the prevailing public opinion.[104]

Another prominent member, Richard Henry Dana, concurred suggesting that the model law might incorporate "alternative provisions" on some points: "[A]t the present the Chicago plan is not understood and it is important, it seems to me, that we do not get the band too far ahead of the procession, that we do not get too far in advance of educated public opinion."[105]

The Illinois delegation argued vigorously against the inclusion of "alternate provisions." Catherwood himself rejected Dana's proposal, in part because of the immorality of "compromising on principles" and in part because the struggle for reform would be more fruitful if advocates of reform could produce "an evidence" of their agreement about desirable reforms:

I think in civil service matters we are apt to lay undue stress on our difficulties, upon our local conditions and the peculiarities of local laws. ... Civil service reform is a great national issue, a place where we have an opportunity to do real patriotic service, and I do not believe in emphasizing difficulties. I think what we want to do, and what we should do, is to get together. ... I believe in making compromises [but] not compromises of principle – when you have a principle, then stick to it and fight for it until you get it settled.[106]

Another member of the model law committee, William Moulton, who was also a member of the Illinois State Commission, agreed with Catherwood about the need to stand firm on the Chicago Plan: "If you are going to adopt a law that you think a legislature will pass, you will never get anywhere. You must come in with an ideal law. ... They may cut off things that they think are important but that may be of no importance; but you must go in with what you think is the ideal measure."[107]

A third member of the model law committee, Ralph Peck of the

Cook County Commission, also urged the assembly to strictly limit variations within the model law:

> The purpose of the investigation of our proposed Standard Act is to be practical and to get practical results before the State Legislatures. It seems to me that if we put up to the State Legislatures various and alternative propositions, your result will be not to procure legislation, but to procure argument and discussion. ... [W]e ought to limit these proposals as closely as we can. ... [W]e ought not now to propose or set up different views of members of this organization.[108]

At the same time, Peck urged the other members of the assembly not to give up on the project of drafting a model law, emphasizing the Illinois delegation's own lobbying problems:

> If we fail to draft any Act here ... they will say: "If you people, if these Civil Service Reform Associations and experts cannot get together, cannot in their expert wisdom frame up a law upon which they may agree, what do you suppose we people down here in the State Legislature are going to do?" ... [S]o far as our people from Illinois are concerned, it is going to aid us materially if we can go to them and take this draft ... and point to the fact that this organization is back of this thing. ... I know the results before the Illinois Assembly are going to be helped a great deal, and I know that our three Commissioners representing Cook County are going to be materially helped.[109]

A member of the Colorado Commission advanced the same line: "[W]hen you go to a Legislature and offer a draft law, they at once ask you: 'What is your authority; you have had no experience in the matter here, you are mere theorists; how are we to find out the experience of older communities?' So that a Model Law is of great importance."[110]

The peculiar thing about the 1916 conference of the National Assembly of Civil Service Commissions was that it was not held in the United States at all, but rather in Ottawa, Canada. The assembly's long, final debate over the model law and its eventual vote to adopt the law much as Catherwood had drafted it were undertaken in the ballroom of the Château Laurier hotel, between receptions at the Governor General's residence and picnics at the government's experimental farm. Canadians who observed the debate were not inclined to think much of it. In fact, a reporter for the *Ottawa Journal* observed:

> At the afternoon session of the Convention the delegates discussed the subject of standard civil service laws. The subject had practically no Canadian interest, relating entirely to standard laws for the examinations etc. of the U.S. Federal, State, and Municipal Commissions. It appears that in the U.S. all the states and cities which are controlled by civil service commissions have different acts, and the present report is an attempt to procure conformity."[111]

The reporter's judgment of the significance of the assembly's deliberations was, unfortunately, badly awry. Canada would shortly become the proving ground for the new model law; in fact, it would be the biggest application of the Chicago Plan anywhere on the continent.

4

The Chicago Plan Comes to Ottawa

Coincidentally, the Canadian government established its own Civil Service Commission at the same time Robert Catherwood was persuading Elton Lower to adopt his "efficiency plan." However, the system established by the Civil Service Act of 1908, which governed the three thousand employees working in departmental headquarters at Ottawa – the "inside service" – differed radically from the regime Catherwood, Griffenhagen and Jacobs would shortly bring to Ottawa.

Before 1915, Canadian civil service reformers, although conscious of the work of American reformers, had looked instead to Britain for a model upon which to base their own efforts at civil service reform. This was the consistent practice of the three royal commissions appointed to study the question of civil service reform between 1881 and 1907.[112] That Canadian reformers should have looked to Britain as an exemplar was not, of course, surprising. Imperialist sentiment was very strong at that time, and the emulation of British civil service practice was part of a broader show of loyalty to what Sir Robert Borden would later call "[the] British connection and British ideals of government."[113] However, the British system was valued for reasons other than its symbolic significance. Inquiries typically noted that the two countries shared "a similar system of government,"[114] and that the British system had proved its practicability through "years of cautious, tentative action."[115]

The main features of the British system were significantly different from those of the Chicago Plan. The British scheme was a highly decentralized one in which senior line officials held sub-stantial discretion over personnel matters. The commission itself was responsible for the administration of entrance examinations for a few service-wide classes and little else. Many departments were permitted to make appointments to lower-level positions without the intervention of the commission. Each department was responsible for the classification of individual positions and its overall staffing plan, subject to the approval of the Treasury. Responsibility for training and advancement of employees was also left with line officials. The success of such a decentralized sys-tem obviously depended upon the quality of the service's senior line officials. In Britain, this managerial class was known as the "first division." These were career appointments recruited pri-marily from Oxford and Cambridge universities.[116]

The Civil Service Act established a crude approximation of the British system.[117] The authority of its new Civil Service Commis-sion was somewhat broader: not only did it administer tests for entrance to service-wide classes, it was also given authority to con-trol promotions within departments. On the other hand, each department was given the authority to classify its own personnel, subject to the approval of classification plans by the Department of Finance and cabinet. The Canadian service also established a "first division," which was to be recruited directly from universities based on academic examinations administered by the Civil Service Commission.

The more senior of the first two civil service commissioners, Adam Shortt, a professor of politics at Queen's University, was also an admirer of the British civil service system. (The second commissioner, Colonel Michel LaRochelle, was clearly also a second fiddle. In September 1908, Shortt wrote to his wife that LaRochelle "seems most anxious to follow my lead and has evi-dently got quite an exalted idea of my capacity in various direc-tions."[118]) A close friend said that Shortt "came to Ottawa with the high purpose of moulding the service into a career for those who should join its ranks, and looked to an ever increasing quota of university graduates. He talked of the Indian service as an ideal, and of the eagerness with which Oxford and Cambridge men, for example, felt honoured in competing under the British system of civil service examinations."[119] The first Canadian civil service examinations, set in May 1909, showed the British influence. While candidates for admission to the lower levels of the civil service were examined in subjects "of the average high school standard" – writing, spelling, arithmetic, geography, history, composition, copying manuscripts, typewriting, stenography and bookkeeping – higher-level examinations were set at a university level and included subjects such as scholastic philosophy, English and French literature, modern languages, the natural sciences, history and economics. The examiners for these tests included faculty members from twelve Canadian universities.[120] The aim was to take a "long and wide view" of governmental problems:

> Write a paper on the *Sphere of the State* [said one question in a 1913 examination] indicating and discussing the chief theories as to what the State ought and ought not to do, and illustrate your answer by contrasting the policies adopted by different epochs: give your opinion, supported by facts, as to the prevailing tendencies of the present day in regard to State interference.[121]

There were, of course, significant obstacles to the implementation of the Civil Service Act, not the least of which was pressure to maintain the patronage system for appointments to the inside service. However, experience showed Shortt that the most persistent lobbying for retention of the patronage system came not from ministers or senior government officials, most of whom were disposed favourably towards the merit system, but from constituency associations whose power was rooted in the ability to withhold nominations from uncooperative members of Parliament. "The forces which operate upon the Government from without," Shortt wrote in private correspondence to the editor of the *Grain Growers' Guide*, "are much more sinister than those which operate upon it from within."[122] In another letter, Shortt explained:

> My experience of nine years as a Commissioner of the Civil Service has revealed to me two aspects of the subject, unappreciated before, first the extent to which the country and the service suffers from the patronage evil and secondly the fact that a considerable majority of Cabinet Ministers and members of Parliament would gladly see the whole system abolished if the general public would actively support

them in this important reform. The greater part of the patronage which prevails, and much the worst part of it is exercised by the local political organizations of both parties, which, because they are instrumental in securing the nominations for the members and claim to be all powerful in securing the elections of the successful candidates, demand that the members and through them the Ministers shall secure positions in the Civil Service and contracts and other economic favours for the persons whom they nominate to them. The members and Ministers are themselves, to a very large extent, only the servants, and often the severely browbeaten servants of organizations from whose thralldom they would most willingly be free, if the independent electors would encourage them to strike for freedom with any hope of permanently maintaining it.[123]

Shortt's view of the character of the patronage problem was quite distinct from that of Robert Catherwood. Catherwood would not have minimized the significance of "the forces within" government, and, in the context of the Chicago experience, he would have been right to do so.

One of the main features that distinguished the Canadian civil service from the Illinois services was the character of the senior non-elected officials who managed the line departments. Although the Canadian deputy ministers were, like Chicago's department heads, "politically appointed" – inasmuch as they were put in their position by cabinet and kept there at cabinet's pleasure – by convention they were not active partisans. In 1914, Sir Joseph Pope, the most senior of Canada's deputy ministers, expressed his understanding of the deputy's function in these terms:

Governments come and go. Even in the same administration changes occur with more or less frequency, but the deputy minister remains. ... Taking no part in politics, the deputy head regards himself as a trustee for the ministry of the day, bound to serve the government in all things so far as he properly can. He is of course bound by a higher sanction to refuse to do, or acquiesce in the doing of, anything contrary to law, or anything which, though not technically illegal, may be opposed to his sense of propriety.[124]

Although this was obviously a hopeful view of the role of Canadian deputies, it was not without some grounding in reality. James Mallory observes: "The old Canadian civil service, with all its faults, had in fact developed a class of administrators who, though uneven in quality, were qualified for higher posts by general ability of a high order."[125] The two dozen deputies had an average of twenty years' experience in the federal service; the great majority had served through several changes of ministry and at least one change of party.[126] In fact, it had been deputy minister of finance John Courtney, "a choleric gentleman ... with a high sense of honour," who had prodded the government of Prime Minister Wilfrid Laurier to action on civil service reform by making an unusual public appeal for the elimination of patronage. Courtney subsequently chaired the commission of inquiry that led to the 1908 Civil Service Act.[127]

The Liberal government, which introduced the Civil Service Act and appointed Shortt as a commissioner, was defeated in the general election of September 1911, but this was not at all a blow for civil service reform. New Conservative Prime Minister Sir Robert Borden had condemned patronage as an "incubus" that "ought to be dealt with in Canada more along the lines on which it is dealt with in England."[128] In January 1912, Borden told Parliament that he intended to proceed with the extension of the Civil Service Act to the "outside service," which comprised the roughly forty thousand federal employees outside of Ottawa, as he had promised in the fall campaign.[129] Borden asked Shortt to prepare a memorandum outlining needed reforms. Shortt complied but urged Borden to appoint a senior British civil servant to study the operation of the Canadian public service. In the summer of 1912, Sir George Murray, a distinguished British administrator who had recently retired as permanent secretary to the Treasury, arrived in Ottawa to begin his work. His report was submitted in November 1912.[130] Although Borden did not agree with all of Murray's recommendations, which covered financial administration and the operation of cabinet as well as management of the civil service, his government did attempt to put into legislation some recommendations regarding the civil service.[131] By 1913–14, however, the government became preoccupied with the debate over naval policy and then the outbreak of war in Europe, and the question of civil service reform was put aside. In a letter to a cabinet colleague, Borden later recalled:

From the summer of 1912, when I went to England, until the end of the following session I was absorbed in our naval proposals and subsequently in negotiations ... as to alternative proposals. Then came the session of 1914 with many difficult and trying questions followed by the outbreak of war. I fear that my attention was almost entirely diverted from any attempt to carry out the pledge of 1907.[132]

Aside from the fact that it did not cover the outside service, and despite the fact that it was severely strained by the expansion of the inside service after the outbreak of war, opinion about the 1908 act seemed generally favourable. Sir George Murray had pronounced it sound in principle, so far as it went.[133] By 1915, the commission considered it safe to delegate its authority over promotion decisions to the deputy ministers and reported "increasing harmony and co-operation" with most departments about appointments to specialized positions in the inside service not governed by the 1908 act.[134] "The system has worked out very satisfactorily," William Foran, secretary of the commission, said in 1915, "We have had practically no complaints about its fairness."[135] On behalf of the deputies, Sir Joseph Pope reported, "There can be little doubt that the [1908 act] has proven on the whole successful. ... Under the skilful guidance of the commission there has been surprisingly little friction, and the public departments have fallen almost imperceptibly into the new order, perhaps the best test of which is to be found in the fact that no one in authority would voluntarily revert to the old conditions of affairs."[136]

THE ADVENT OF THE CHICAGO PLAN

The most senior civil servant within the Canadian Civil Service Commission was its secretary, William Foran. In 1915, Foran was forty-seven years old, and he already had thirty-two years' experience in the federal service. He joined the service as a temporary employee in 1887 and worked his way into a permanent position as a third-class clerk in the Department of the Secretary of State. He was appointed as secretary of the old Board of Civil Service Examiners in 1896 and took the analogous position in the new Civil Service Commission in 1908. By then he was ranked in subdivision A of the first division of the civil service, the highest position possible for a career employee.[137] By all accounts, Foran had a sharp wit, a keen grasp of governmental procedure and a remarkable dedication to his work. Foran "was more than the secretary of the Civil Service Commission," the *Ottawa Journal* said on his retirement in 1939,

> In much of the public mind, he was the Commission, Foran stood by the Commission's cradle, watched it grow through forty years, championed it and fought for it against all comers, knew more about it and its aims and work than anybody else. ... Once a parliamentary committee ... advised Foran to confine himself to "the duties of a secretary." The advice was as sensible – and as effective – as King Canute's efforts with the waves. ... Foran could no more be a mere Secretary to the Commission than the skipper of a ship could be a cabin boy.[138]

When, in early 1915, the Civil Service Commission received an invitation from the National Assembly of Civil Service Commissions to send a delegate to their next convention in Los Angeles, it must have seemed obvious to Foran that he should attend. Quickly he persuaded the two commissioners that "it would be in the interests of the Public Service, and more particularly of this Commission" to have its secretary go to the conference. Certainly Foran overcame significant obstacles to attend the Los Angeles conference: it took eight days by train to get there, and when he returned, a Treasury Board official refused to cover his expenses, arguing that it was not policy to reimburse expenses for conferences held outside of Canada.[139]

Why did the assembly extend an invitation to the Canadian commissioners? Once again, the answer probably lies in its members' problems in fighting for reform in their own jurisdictions. The president of the assembly, F.E. Doty of the Los Angeles County Commission, said after the meeting that the presence of a representative of the Canadian commission, "whose members are appointed for life, served to give additional support to the demand for security of tenure for commissioners on this side of the border."[140] The assembly probably also believed that the representation of another national commission would add lustre to the reputation of an organization that was otherwise comprised almost entirely of state and local officials. This would explain the surprisingly warm reception that was given to Foran: even though he was new to the assembly, Foran was featured as the opening speaker at the 1915 conference and was immediately named as one of the three members of the assembly's executive committee. Foran reciprocated by inviting the assembly to hold its 1916 meeting in Ottawa. Thus it was that the final debate over the assembly's model law, which culminated in the assembly's endorsement of the Chicago Plan, came to be held in the Château Laurier hotel.

As a senior public servant, Foran considered himself precluded from speaking publicly on the subject of civil service reform, and consequently Adam Shortt was the only Canadian to participate in the debates at the 1916 meeting. Shortt was less enthusiastic than Foran about the assembly's work; in fact, his main contribution to the 1916 debates was an argument against Catherwood's proposal to use "efficiency ratings" to control promotions and dismissals within the civil service. "No mathematical processes or rules," Shortt argued, could eliminate the need to rely on the "personal judgement" of department heads who had a better understanding of their employees' talents than a Civil Service Commission could hope to possess. "The executive heads will give a good judgement," Shortt argued, "As a rule they are not over-awed by their political heads." As to the work Catherwood had already completed on efficiency records, Shortt observed: "The experiments that have been made ... strike me as very desirable even if they are not productive of successful results. Carlyle, in the preparation of his history of Frederick the Great, after wading through a dozen or two volumes occupying a week or two would say: 'At least that proves there is nothing there.'"[141]

Shortt's argument in favour of the trustworthiness of line managers was directed at the foundation of Catherwood's argument in favour of the model law, but there is no evidence that it had any impact at all. It seems, in fact, that Shortt's comments were politely disregarded. Hardly had Shortt finished speaking when Richard Henry Dana, one of the most pre-eminent members of the assembly, asked his colleagues:

> Do we not, after all labour most under this difficulty, that the real head of the Department – I do not mean the Cabinet member who

aids the Government in deciding the general policies – but the head of the operative department who carries out those policies when they are determined upon, is put in for political reasons and his effort is to do the best that he can for his party, not for the efficiency of the department? If he can raise the salary of somebody who is a friend of a politician or a good party worker from his point of view, that is his duty, is it not, as a politician? If he can get a good many positions with high salaries exempted, that is his political duty – and that is not much of an inspiration to the employees under him, is it?[142]

While the Ottawa meeting of the national assembly might have frustrated Adam Shortt, there is no doubt that it was a personal triumph for William Foran. The *Ottawa Journal* boasted that Foran had brought to Ottawa "many of the most brainy of ... commission officials"; it reported that the Château Laurier's Palm Room, its walls decorated with entwined British and American flags, "throbbed with brotherly love." The American delegates restrained their democratic impulses long enough to wait enthusiastically upon the Duke of Connaught, the Governor General and uncle of the King. At the end of it all, the assembly elected Foran as its president for 1917. The *Ottawa Journal* professed its surprise, reporting that it had been "generally understood" that New York's Henry Moskowitz would be given the position[143]; but perhaps Moskowitz's prospects were clouded by his opposition to Catherwood's model law. Foran accepted the position humbly: "When I recall the list of very able men who have filled this office since the establishment of the Assembly I realize that my duties are by no means light, that they have set a standard which it will require my best efforts to live up to. But I can assure you that, while I am President of this Assembly, no efforts on my part shall be wanting to maintain that standard."[144]

The Opportunity for Reform

Some time later, Foran had an opportunity to call upon the assembly for help in reorganizing the Canadian service. In August 1917, the Borden government introduced conscription for military service. Conscription was strongly opposed by many Canadians, including most French Canadians. In a bid to maintain popular support, Borden formed a coalition government of Conservatives and anglophone Liberals and called a federal election for December 17. Borden also made a commitment to the elimination of patronage in the outside service one of the main planks in the new government's platform. On October 18, he issued a manifesto promising to "abolish patronage" by "extending the principle of the present Civil Service Act to the Outside Service."[145] Aside from establishing the selflessness of the new Union government, this promise solved an immediate practical problem. Minister of trade and commerce Sir George Foster observed that one of the great difficulties of the Union government was getting Liberals and Conservatives in each riding "to fraternize and cooperate." "The flaming matter of patronage" – the question of who would dole out favours in each riding – could tear the coalition apart. But if patronage was eliminated the prospects for cooperation were much improved.[146]

It is probably not surprising that Borden made his commitment to abolish patronage without considering how it was to be accomplished. Only a few days before issuing his October manifesto, Borden asked the civil service commissioners to

> make an immediate inquiry into the details necessary for extending the Civil Service Act to all branches of the public service including the Outside Service. It seems to me that the time has come when this should be accomplished. Probably it may necessitate the establishment of ancillary local boards in various parts of the Dominion. Such Boards would be under the direction of the Central Commission and should make necessary reports for the purpose of determining appointments.[147]

The commissioners, in turn, called a meeting of deputy ministers at the Victoria Museum, to ensure their "sympathetic cooperation" and to "obtain opinions of men of considerable experience ... as to the practicability of the project." The deputies were pessimistic in their assessment of the situation. New legislation would be required, and there would be impressive administrative and political obstacles to be overcome:

> That the Outside Service can be brought under the Civil Service Commission was, generally speaking, the consensus of opinion. ...

That to do so with one sweep of the pen would involve great difficulty, is beyond question. ... In general, the bringing in of the Outside Service will involve much difficulty and annoyance to the Government and the new members thereof, extending over, not only months, but years.

The commissioners suggested a gradual program of reform, beginning with more senior positions in the outside service and then proceeding to lower positions.[148]

The commissioners' report seemed to have no influence on Borden; in fact, a few days later the prime minister issued a second manifesto promising an immediate end to patronage in the outside service. But the cabinet did nothing more to consider how the promise would be put into place. Borden himself was preoccupied with the campaign, while Alexander Maclean, the minister whom he had asked to handle the report, was preoccupied with a munitions explosion that had devastated his Halifax constituency. "The C.S. Board has done nothing yet," Sir George Foster lamented in his diary after a cabinet meeting on January 23, a month after the re-election of the Union government. "[It has] had no instructions. Appts meantime go on as before via the path of patronage in all but Inside Service. Will the Premier repeat the 1911–17 methods of fulfilling his promises? The same influences which stopped him then are discernable now – will he yield again?"[149]

The pressure on Borden to take action on reform of the outside service was mounting quickly. In many constituencies, Conservative associations were beginning to dispense patronage, creating an embarrassment for the prime minister and putting a serious strain on the new Union government. The parliamentary Opposition and the press, particularly incensed by two high-profile appointments, were claiming that Borden had no intention of abolishing patronage. Foster wrote in his diary that the two appointments "have stirred up a wide strong feeling that good faith has not been kept. The two appts were made in the face of a solemn pledge to the contrary and have brought criticism and obloquy on the Govt and party."[150] The chairman of the union committee in Toronto warned Borden that there was "serious danger that the principle of patronage being continued will weaken the confidence of the community in the Union Government unless it is stopped speedily."[151]

By late January 1918, Borden realized that immediate action was essential. It was impossible to introduce new legislation because none had been drafted and Parliament was not scheduled to meet until March. Borden decided that, in the interim, reforms would be introduced by regulation, even though it was "extremely doubtful" that the government had authority under any statute to make such regulations. The regulation, issued on February 13, announced that the patronage system would be abolished in the outside service.[152] The regulation did not say, however, how the system that was to take its place would work. The responsibility for these details was now left to the Civil Service Commission, as the cabinet moved on to other business.

The commissioners must have been boggled by the magnitude of the task that had just been put to them. In February 1918, the commission's staff consisted of eight clerks headquartered in a small suite of offices over a haberdashery on the corner of Bank and Queen streets. The commissioners themselves were, furthermore, new to the task. Adam Shortt had resigned from the commission before the election, and two new commissioners – Clarence Jameson and William Roche – were appointed to replace him in October.[153] The circumstances combined to give the commission's secretary, William Foran, substantial influence in deciding how the reform of the outside service should be handled. Foran, in turn, called on Robert Catherwood for help because he knew him to be one of the most highly regarded U.S. experts on reform.[154]

Catherwood recommended that the Canadian commission hire Edwin Griffenhagen to execute the reforms. Griffenhagen had left Chicago's South Park Commission in 1911 to become head of a new management consulting branch set up by Arthur Young and Company, a Chicago-based accounting firm. For the six years following, Griffenhagen's industrial engineering department had provided advice to a variety of midwestern businesses, such as the Oklahoma Iron Works, Milwaukee Seed and the Chicago Steel Post Company. Although he had continued to promote the Chicago Plan at meetings of the National Assembly of Civil Service Commissions, contracts from public organizations had been hard to come by; it is probable that the Illinois Pension Laws Commission was the only significant governmental client whom he had served in all these years.[155] The Canadian contract was, therefore, a wonderful opportunity. In fact, it would shortly be recognized as the largest single effort at civil service reform yet undertaken by any government. Griffenhagen and a staff of twenty-seven began working on the reform of the Canadian service in the spring of 1918.[156]

The Chicago Plan is Installed

The system Griffenhagen and his staff installed in Canada included all the main features of the assembly's model law. In November 1918, Griffenhagen's principal assistant, Fred Telford, unveiled a new design for the Civil Service Commission that included an "organization branch" whose mandate would be to conduct efficiency investigations within the public service.[157] (Telford was a recent addition to Griffenhagen's staff. A former country schoolteacher, Telford had worked for eighteen months as an assistant examiner for the Illinois civil service commissioner and then briefly as a reporter for Chicago's *Civil Service News*.[158]) Griffenhagen said the functions of the organization branch were "almost identical" with those of the Chicago commission's efficiency division.[159] In its annual report for 1918, the Canadian commission defined the branch's field of study in a passage that was taken almost verbatim from Robert Catherwood's 1913 speech to the National Assembly of Civil Service Commissions:

> The prompt and automatic removal of incompetents and supernumeraries, the correction and adjustment of defective organization, the steady improvement of conditions of employment, the training of employees in their duties and for promotion, the task of keeping competent employees in their duties and for promotion, the task of keeping competent employees, the correlation of pay with the results achieved, the preparation of estimates in their employment features as distinguished from their financial aspects, and the maintenance of standards of efficient service are all problems of employment with which the merit system deals.[160]

The commission announced its intention to make "liberal and considered use" of the branch, noting that while it hoped to have the cooperation of the departments, the branch would be "[armed] with inquisitorial power when the occasion may demand."[161]

The commission also took on the same regulatory powers over personnel that had been exercised by the Chicago commission and recommended in the model law. New legislation confirming the commission's authority to classify positions, set salaries and to control promotions, transfers and dismissals was put before the House of Commons in June 1919. A plan, which described the new classifications for positions in the public service, was released a few days later.[162] This first draft, popularly known as the "Book of Classification," ran to almost seven hundred pages and described 1,729 classifications – roughly one class for every twenty federal employees.[163]

Meanwhile, the commission proceeded with the development of a system for "efficiency rating" of individual employees. It described its ambitions for the efficiency rating system in a pamphlet for employees:

> The rating of an individual must as far as possible eliminate personal prejudice, or what might be called the variation of the human equation, which occurs when even the most conscientious of men is asked to give his written opinion and recommendation concerning a number of persons with whom he has had more or less personal relations. This is the object of the "numerical" or "percentage" system, whereby the efficiency of an applicant can be expressed in arithmetical terms capable of mathematical weights and comparison.[164]

5

The Deputies' Rebellion

Far from going "unnoticed or unlamented," as the Glassco Commission would later claim, the burdens created by the Chicago Plan were immediately apparent to senior officials within the government and provoked an intense debate between the commission and those officials. By late 1919, in fact, many deputy ministers had begun a quiet lobby for major changes to the new civil service laws. Griffenhagen and the commission's staff, however, were consistently reluctant to concede any of the powers the 1918 and 1919 acts had now given it.

CIVIL SERVANTS PROTEST

The release of the "Book of Classification" in June 1919 actually threw the civil service into disarray almost immediately. The political scientist, R. McGregor Dawson, then working in the parliamentary library, recalled that the "the whole service was in an uproar."[165] Civil servants struggled, without much success, to understand how the classifications had been developed and how their own positions had been classified. Departmental "checking lists," which showed the new classification of individual employees, might have answered the latter question, but Griffenhagen and his staff, rushing to release the "Book of Classification" before the adjournment of Parliament at the end of June, had not had time to complete them.[166] A few top civil servants knew their new classifications, one disgruntled civil servant complained, but "the remainder of the service, which probably amounts to 97 per cent. of it, are in absolute ignorance of where they stand."[167]

Civil servants who wanted to know what their new salary might be were therefore obliged to search the "Book of Classification" itself and guess which classification might cover their own position. Unfortunately, copies of the book were hard to come by. "There is probably no way in which you could get a copy for your own use," the commission helpfully advised one civil servant, "though every department head and the head of every large branch has a copy, to which employees undoubtedly will be given access."[168] (The commission claimed it had only printed a few copies of the book because it expected that many revisions would need to be made. Rumour said that the commission, surprised by the protest against the book, had "whisked away" all the copies it could find and burned them.)[169]

If a copy of the book could be found, the next challenge was to sort through the 1,729 classifications to find the one which seemed to best describe the employee's own position. In earlier American classification plans, the practice had been to group similar classifications together so that readers would have an easier time finding their classification or seeing potential lines of advancement, or to provide an appendix that divided classifications into groups or "services." Griffenhagen chose not to organize the book in this way; such groups, he later said, "were not an essential part" of a classification plan.[170] Instead, classes were listed in alphabetical order by title so that similar classifications were dispersed throughout the book. For example, the description for "chief clerk" appeared near the front while the closely related classification of "principal clerk" appeared several hundred pages further on. Not even knowing the titles of the new classifications, civil servants were compelled to slog through the whole book to guess where they might fit. The book "is about as clear as mud," a columnist in *The Citizen* in Ottawa complained two days after its release. "Careful perusal by the average individual results in as clear a conception of its intricacies as 'Bosco' the wild man possesses of the Fourth Dimension."[171] A member of Parliament agreed: "No intelligent man can understand all of the seven hundred page volume ... it is a catalogue with the most curious and unintelligible classifications for certain positions that I have ever seen."[172] A leader of the Civil Service Association of Ottawa later called the plan "a monstrosity, a book of mystery, a monument to the fecundity of the human mind," that should be "put on the shelf in some museum, so that members of the Civil Service Commission could make a pilgrimage to the shrine as a punishment for their folly in bringing foreign experts into this country."[173]

Layered on top of this confusion were widespread questions about the methods Griffenhagen and his staff had used to craft particular classifications and to determine the salaries attached to each of them. These, again, could only be answered by speculation because the report that was to explain how the plan was developed had also been put aside in the rush to complete the book itself. This speculation often led to the expression of doubts about the reliability of the plan and of Griffenhagen's own competence. "I thought these Civil Service experts were fixing salaries in accordance with responsibilities," a postal worker wrote to the *Ottawa Journal* on June 26. "There is very clearly something wrong with these classifications."[174] The next day, another complained that "he did not think the experts had sufficient knowledge" of the positions they had classified.[175] Yet another complained about the haphazard way in which Griffenhagen and his staff had conducted their investigations:

> Instead of visiting the departments and offices and, as far as possible, acquiring a first hand knowledge of affairs, they took their information from a card index. Instead of calling all deputy ministers and heads of branches and consulting with them, and thus getting a fully orbed view of Civil Service operations, they called only a few, or depended on volunteer information. ... It is easy to see that by this method they would get a distorted view ... of the importance of some individuals and branches. ... [I]t is evident that the classification needs considerable revision yet before it is adopted; and it is also evident that the work of fitting it to the present staff should be put in the hands of someone who knows the men and the conditions, if gross injustice is to be avoided.[176]

Soon others were making fun of the classification scheme calling it "the joke book" or "the best book of short stories in the English language."[177] A column satirizing the "Book of Classification" appeared on the front page of the *Ottawa Journal*:

> Question: I am a Burroughs Adding Machine. The idiot that bangs my keys every day receives $1,400. What should I get?

> Answer: The Civil Service re-organizers are unfortunately not able to overcome some of the prejudices by which men are preferred to machines. Otherwise you would receive about $3,600 under the application of the principle of equal pay for equal work.[178]

Complaints about the superficiality of Griffenhagen's investigation did, in fact, have some grounding to them. Hoping to speed up the process of classification, Griffenhagen had taken two "short cuts" in procedure. His normal practice had been to ask every employee to complete "duties statements" that described "their regular duties, the apportionment of their time to the several items of work, and their place in the organization." In Canada, however, Griffenhagen chose not to poll every employee; where superiors said a group of employees all did the same work, only one or two received questionnaires. The classification staff was also accustomed to completing field studies to confirm the accuracy of the data collected and their classifications; in Canada this work was curtailed as well.[179]

Civil servants who took more time to examine the "Book of Classification" also expressed concerns about the provisions it had made for promotion within the service. Griffenhagen's staff had attached to each classification a short list of positions into which incumbents might expect promotion. Many classifications, ranging from the bottom to the top of the service, were chained together in this way. Civil servants who looked closely at these "lines of promotion," as Griffenhagen called them, wondered about their workability: how, for example, was a clerk to be promoted to the next position of senior clerk when the former required only a primary school education and the latter a high school education? The fact was that Griffenhagen could not give strong assurances about the workability of the scheme because he had never actually tried it before. The promotion system was, as Griffenhagen said, "a refinement not hitherto attempted in classification work."[180] He appears to have taken the idea from an article on shop management published by the efficiency engineers, Frank and Lillian Gilbreth, in 1915.[181]

Protests against the classification became so intense in the two weeks following its release that the Borden government delayed parliamentary consideration of the new civil service legislation until the fall session of Parliament. It did this reluctantly because in the summer of 1919 there were, in its eyes, far more important things to worry about. The prime minister had left for Versailles while acting prime minister Sir George Foster was struggling to hold together the Union government and to contain widespread labour unrest. The commission was given the summer to respond to the civil service's complaints.

The commission's reaction to the protests was not a friendly one. Shortly after the adjournment of Parliament, Foran chastised civil servants for criticizing the report:

> The classification of the Public Service of Canada was a task which might reasonably have occupied from eighteen to twenty-four months. Owing to the desire of the Government to meet the wishes of the Service, however, the Civil Service Commission rushed the work through in about eight months. That some errors and anomalies should appear in certain of the sixteen hundred odd schedules is not, in the circumstances, to be wondered.[182]

A little later the commission suggested that the bulk of criticisms were coming from "malcontents ... a comparatively small minority, viewing [the classification] from the selfish angle of personal application."[183] It urged civil servants to have patience as its "body of trained experts" completed the departmental checking lists and heard appeals against individual classifications.[184] At the commission's suggestion, another efficiency expert, Louis Jacobs, was brought to Ottawa to provide a second opinion about the classification work. It seems doubtful that many of the public servants who gathered in Ottawa's Collegiate Institute in the evening of July 4 to hear Jacobs knew that he had once worked with Griffenhagen in the efficiency division of the Chicago Civil Service Commission.[185]

The commission's early response to civil service complaints soon proved to be wholly inadequate. By mid-July, two major employees' associations – the Dominion Postal Clerks' Association and the Great War Veterans' Association – had come out against the classification,[186] while the members of a third – the Civil Service Association of Ottawa – were mobilizing to throw out its executive, which had spoken in favour of the reforms.[187] The executive of the Civil Service Federation of Canada, a loose association of employee organizations, had also been favourably disposed towards the reforms, but by early July it too was obliged to shift its position. It told Borden that it had voted to "[refrain] from expressing its sentiments in favour of the immediate adoption of the Government's classification report."[188]

THE DEPUTIES PROTEST

Meanwhile, the deputy ministers, to whom the commission had said complaints should be addressed, were becoming increasingly angry about the experts' management of the classification. On July 29, commissioner Clarence Jameson chaired a conference at the Victoria Museum at which Griffenhagen and the staff of the organization branch were called to account by fifty senior officials from line departments.[189] The officials demanded that departments should be allowed to make their own checking lists, and that a special "board of hearing" should be set up to hear employees' appeals. The proposed board would include representatives of the deputy heads and the employees' associations, but exclude the experts.

The experts refused to go along with the proposal for a board of hearing; they preferred a grievance process that gave the Civil Service Commission's staff the final say on complaints. Griffenhagen would not waver from this position. One senior official recalled that there was "a battle royal with the Arthur Young Company before we were able to lay unholy hands on the classification which they had prepared."[190] At the end of the day, however, the deputies were aided by a rift that was emerging within the commission itself. Clarence Jameson, one of the two members of Parliament who had been appointed to the commission in October 1917, was losing patience with Griffenhagen and eventually submitted to the deputies' request for a special board to review the "Book of Classification."[191]

Jameson told the press that the new Board of Hearing was intended to "establish confidence on the part of the members of the service in the endeavour of the Civil Service Commission, to make the classification as accurate as possible ... [and to] secure if possible its adoption at the autumn session of Parliament." The board would have five members: Jameson, two deputies and two civil servants – all men who were, as Jameson put it, "trained in and thoroughly acquainted with the service." Experts from either Arthur Young and Company or the commission itself would not be put on the panel.[192] The symbolic effect of the board's work was substantial. It was "cheering news," the president of the Civil Service Federation said, to see that the commission had recognized the need for "drastic action" on the "Book of Classification."[193] "If it had not been for the Board of Hearing," another federation leader later said, "the present Civil Service Act would not have been on the Statute books ... it afforded an opportunity for groups of civil servants to come before the board and make their complaint. It relieved the Commission, and it relieved the Government, and in that way I think established very mutual good will in the days of stress of 1918–1919–1920."[194]

This was the most public tussle between deputies and the experts, but it was not the first. Complaints about the commission's inability to manage the workload created under the Chicago Plan had been voiced since Griffenhagen's arrival in Ottawa in early 1918. In March 1918, deputy minister of finance John Saunders, asked the commission to provide his department with staff "at once" to organize the 1918 Victory Loan drive. The commission insisted on running a national, two-month competition for the positions. The minister "got very hot" and told Saunders to break the law so that the staff could be hired in time.[195] The deputy minister of the new Department of Soldiers' Civil Re-Establishment also complained that the commission's selection process was "altogether too slow."[196] The commission's staff expanded rapidly in an attempt to manage the work the reforms had created for it – in 1921 the commission employed more people in Ottawa than most other government departments[197] – but these complaints about its slowness persisted.

As time passed, complaints about the commission's interference in the management of line departments also accumulated. Adam

Shortt was one of the first to complain about the new regime, perhaps because he knew better than most what it was intended to do. Shortt, now working in a new position at the National Archives, had expressed a worry about the design of the new system in private correspondence in January 1918:

> It is of course essential that any system of Civil Service Reform shall be sound in principle and workable in practice, allowing all necessary freedom to those who are working for efficiency and the recognition of merit in the department, while affording effectual and practicable checks on the conduct of those whose chief object it is to support and manipulate a patronage system.[198]

Two months later, Shortt began to see that the system Griffenhagen and Foran were installing would not strike the balance between principle and practicality. At the end of March, he wrote to the commission to advise that he had found a person whom he wanted to hire as a research assistant. Shortt's selection was Charlotte Whitton, a recent double medallist at Queen's University who would eventually become mayor of Ottawa.[199] William Foran refused to appoint Whitton, saying that the commission would run an open competition and appoint its own board of experts to choose the best candidate for Shortt's position. This was a significant change from the commission's policy under Shortt but one entirely consistent with the Chicago Plan. Shortt was infuriated and complained to Sir George Foster who was acting as prime minister in Robert Borden's absence:

> I have just been informed that the Civil Service Commission has adopted the extraordinary principle, that in making its selection of candidates to fill technical, professional or other positions requiring special qualifications, no persons shall be consulted who has immediate charge of the work to be performed. ... Applying the new principle to your own department, if for instance, Mr. Coats were authorized by you to obtain, through the Civil Service Commission, the assistance of a person with special qualifications including those personal qualities so essential to success, what would you think of a system of selection which not only eliminated Mr. Coats from all consultation by the Commission as to the choice, but prevented him

from even knowing who were the candidates and what were their respective qualifications, yet Mr. Coats is entirely responsible for the assistant assigned to him? I cannot think of anything more calculated to injure the cause of Civil Service Reform or to render its practical operation ridiculous, than this attitude of the Commission, adopted I presume with very good intentions, but with a lamentable disregard of the very elements of economy and efficiency.[200]

In a letter that again echoed the words of the Chicago reformers, Foran refused to budge, telling Shortt that the new hiring procedure "is absolutely fair and just and is calculated to allay any suspicion which might otherwise exist that in these cases some particular applicant is likely to be favoured by the officials of the Department to which the appointment is to be made."[201]

Senior officials soon developed other criticisms of the new system. The deputy minister of labour complained that the new classification plan was "cumbersome and tedious, lacking in any feature of elasticity and opposed generally to the expedition, efficiency and economy."[202] "You can not operate your staff," agreed the deputy minister of public works, whose department had been divided into 327 classes, "there is no elasticity. Take a person whose duties are described as so and so or such and such; his duties must be very similar to those of some person in the next room. But probably a sentence was added to the definition of his duties, and you cannot transfer [him to that other person's job]. ... There is no way of utilizing your staff where they are most needed. You cannot get the same punch to your staff."[203]

The deputies complained not only about the delays in making appointments and promotions, but also about the commission's competence in making these decisions. The under-secretary of state pined for the days when, "If I wanted to get a lawyer ... [I would] go to the Dean of McGill University law school, or the Principal of Osgoode Hall and ask him to pick out two or three that I could interview."[204] John Saunders wondered how there could be "anyone outside the department who knows the qualifications for promotion like the man who is in charge of the work which the man is to be promoted is doing."[205] Deputy minister of the interior, William Cory added that the new system was also a source of unending paperwork:

I happened to go down [to the mailroom one day], and I found 56 letters there, [including] 33 from the Civil Service Commission. ... I called in one of my staff the next morning and I asked if that was about how the mail was running, and he said, "Yes", so we kept track of it for about eight or ten months. ... Here is the result. ... During that time [we received] from the Civil Service Commission, 2,711 [letters], as against 2,398 from the rest of the world. ... The outgoing mail ... 2,652 communications going to the Civil Service Commission ... as against 4,242 [to the rest of the world]. Practically 50 per cent of the time of the deputy minister's staff, as far as correspondence is concerned, is taken up with the Civil Service Commission.[206]

As a concession to the deputies, Clarence Jameson had, in the summer of 1919, exempted ten thousand lower-level positions from the Civil Service Act, but this was not enough to quiet complaints. In the same year, John Saunders of Finance sought special legislation that exempted loan drive staff from the Civil Service Act,[207] and Samuel Armstrong of the Department of Soldiers' Civil Re-Establishment obtained legislation that exempted all four thousand of his employees from the act. In the fall of 1919, deputy minister of justice Edmund Newcombe, even took the unusual step of appearing before a Senate committee to "strongly attack" the new legislation, creating for a moment a popular impression that the bill might be killed.[208] (The possibility of any such revolt in the House had been precluded by Alexander Maclean, the minister responsible for the bill, who chaired the committee himself and who permitted three witnesses: Griffenhagen, Telford and one other member of Griffenhagen's staff.[209]) In the spring of 1920, the High Commission in London also began lobbying the prime minister to exempt it from the act on the argument that the Civil Service Commission was incapable of competently managing personnel in London.[210]

Many deputies soon began a more concerted campaign to persuade Prime Minister Arthur Meighen, who had replaced Sir Robert Borden as head of the Liberal–Conservative coalition in July 1920, to introduce legislation that would restore to them some of the powers now held by the commission. In the spring of 1921, the Meighen government acquiesced, sponsoring a bill that would loosen the commission's control over appointments and promotions. Minister of justice Charles Doherty made the remarkable concession that the commission did not support the amendments:

I believe it would be fair to say that they were opposing them. I would judge by what I have seen of newspaper utterances that the Civil Service Commission take the position ... that whatever complaint may be made, whatever suggestions of possible improvements may be made, the Civil Service Act stands there like the Ark of the Covenant upon which no man, especially no member of Parliament, and least of all the Parliament of Canada, must lay an unholy hand. I do not think that is an unfair description of the position taken by the Civil Service Commission.[211]

Doherty's deputy, Edmund Newcombe, the first witness before the parliamentary committee set up to consider the bill, testified that the commission's insistence on control over personnel matters had led to "embarrassment, loss of time, and difficulty in carrying out the essential services."[212] He was followed by ten other deputies who voiced similar complaints. The committee itself concluded that "there is a genuine desire on the part of deputy heads ... to adhere to the idea of a Civil Service Commission ... having regard for the efficiency of the service and economy in expenditure," and it broadly approved of more liberal rules on appointments and promotions.

However, there was by this time little hope that the government would adopt such amendments. Its bill had been attacked from the start as "the thin edge of the wedge in returning to the spoils system,"[213] and even before the hearings had begun many major newspapers had editorialized against it. The scope of the bill was limited dramatically, ultimately giving the commission the power to exempt certain classes of employees where it considered such exemptions to be in the public interest. However, the commission did not escape completely unscathed. One employees' association, which had opposed the bill during parliamentary hearings, also condemned the commission and its experts for having provoked it:

When the commission in its ignorance and helplessness engaged the Arthur Young Company to reclassify the service, that eminent firm adopted an attitude of almost impudent disregard of any representations made, even by the highest and most responsible departmental officers; any one of their employees knew far more about the work of a department than the deputy minister of that department himself. The Civil Service Commission, by continuing to show an autocratic disregard of departmental recommendations, by unreasonable delays in making appointments, and even in handling the merest routine, by their unwillingness to show the slightest cooperation with departments with a view to prompt and satisfactory administration of the service, by piling regulation on regulation in the attempt to coerce the service into their idea of efficiency ... has alienated the truest friends of the merit system and has now placed that system itself in the gravest danger.[214]

Undeterred by the defeat of the 1921 bill, the deputies continued their fight for new legislation. In June 1921, Sir Joseph Pope asked the High Commission in London to collect information about the regulations that governed the British civil service, and some time later John Saunders dispatched one of his own subordinates to London to make an investigation of the British administration.[215] A new Liberal government under Prime Minister William Lyon Mackenzie King was elected in December 1921, and the deputies shortly renewed their lobby of the cabinet. In June 1922, the deputies held an unusual meeting *en masse* with King's cabinet to make a "full and frank expression of their views" about the commission.[216] King asked William Cory, deputy minister of the interior, to organize a committee to draft suggestions for reform of the Civil Service Act. A week later, Sir Joseph Pope wrote to Cory:

> The present unconstitutional, cumbrous and hugely expensive system should be done away with as soon as circumstances permit. The power to classify and promote and also to regulate salaries should be resumed by the Government. To the Commission might be left the application of certain tests, and also of ascertaining the qualifications of those whom the Government proposes to promote, though as a matter of fact, I believe the Deputy Heads are much better judges of such fitness than any Civil Service Commission.[217]

In December, Cory's committee submitted a memorandum requesting statutory changes that would replace the 1919 classification with a simpler classification "on lines similar to those established by the Civil Service Act of 1908" and eliminate the commission's control over appointments to higher-level positions, promotions and transfers. The committee of deputies argued that these reforms would *"eliminate expensive services* which are wholly concerned in the making and enforcing of *artificial requirements* regulating appointments, promotions, [and] transfers."[218] In February 1923, the King government appointed a second parliamentary committee to review the Civil Service Act.

The 1923 hearings were much more extensive than those of 1921 but hardly more productive. The commission again opposed substantial modifications to its powers. Its experts had already dismissed the 1908 act as one that was "inadequate," "haphazard," and "administered ... without regard for sound and scientific employment principles." Griffenhagen's reforms, the commission said, had "revolutionized the service" and wrought "order out of chaos."[219] The deputies' efforts were also impeded by the popular interpretation of the investigation as a return to the patronage system. "The pressing problem," Adam Shortt wrote to William Grant, "is to get the system back to a simple, solid, understandable basis on the British model instead of on the present pretentious trashy American model and to do that without the abolition of the whole system and restore primitive patronage. ... If only [we] could get someone like Sir George Murray to re-state the British principles and practice it would greatly help."[220] In fact, civil service leaders claimed that Civil Service Commission staff was actively promoting the view that any modification of the Civil Service Act would be tantamount to a reversion to patronage:

> Attempts are being made, through articles in the press, editorials, interviews with members, etc., etc., to create the impression in the minds of the House that the preservation of the merit system in the service and the retention of the present Civil Service Commission and its methods, are synonymous, that there is only one alternative, either to preserve the present Civil Service Commission and its methods, or to resort to patronage in its most objectionable and shameless form.[221]

The argument, which was apparently being made by Civil Service

Commission staff, was again strongly reminiscent of one made by Robert Catherwood to the Assembly of Civil Service Commissions.[222] It seems to have been effective in putting off legislative action; after three months of hearings the parliamentary committee made an unusually brief and tepid comment on the deputies' complaints:

> [The] Committee feel that [the deputies'] report was conceived for the sole purpose of promoting efficiency in the Civil Service, yet it cannot but feel that the Commissioners are *bona fide* in their objections to the report. [The] Committee recommends that at the earliest possible date a conference toward greater efficiency be held between the Commissioners and the deputy ministers for the purpose of arriving at an understanding over the matters therein set out.[223]

Such a conference appears never to have been held.

The commission did, however, make one final and important concession to the deputy ministers. There was still the question of how it would manage its organization branch – the Canadian analogue to Chicago's efficiency division, which at that point had been defunct for more than four years. The commission had recruited a chief for the organization branch in July 1919. The advertisement explained that the commission wanted an individual with "at least five years experience in accounting, engineering, shop and business management, or similar work" to "conduct investigations into departmental affairs with a view to making the civil service efficient."[224] An examination for the position was set shortly after. One question asked candidates: "Explain briefly your idea of the meaning of five of the following terms: Standardization, unit cost, efficiency, time and motion study, layout, production control, cost accounting."[225]

However, the commission's keenness to use the "inquisitorial power" that had been vested in the organization branch soon waned. The branch did, in fact, give memoranda to the government that outlined "the more obvious possibilities of reducing the cost of civil administration at Ottawa": through the reorganization of branches within and among departments, amalgamation of whole departments, centralization of services to line departments, and consolidation of government offices.[226] But it became apparent that detailed investigations along these lines would inflame relations with the deputies, and the commissioners shortly refused to exercise their legal authority unless invited to make an investigation by a line department or expressly directed to make one by cabinet. Few invitations came, and no such directions were ever issued.[227]

6

The Reformers' Rhetoric: Its Effects

With the benefit of hindsight we can easily see the mistake that precipitated the battle between the deputies and the commission between 1918 and 1923. The system that had been installed in the Canadian service was designed for a different kind of government: most notably, one in which senior line officials were partisans and very often corrupt too. The Canadian deputies were not politicized in the same way as were their Chicagoan counterparts, and they were generally not corrupt. The Canadian system, unlike the Chicago system, did not need to be made "burglar proof."

Why was this important difference not noted in the 1918–23 debate? And why were the efficiency experts – whether those within Arthur Young and Company or those within the commission's new organization branch – so obstinate in their refusal to accommodate senior officials who complained about the burdens imposed by the new system? The answer to these questions may be found by examining the rhetorical strategy, which reformers in Chicago had invented and which had been brought to Canada by the expert community in 1918. After all, the experts themselves were hardly quiet in the years 1918–23. As senior officials, lower-level employees and members of Parliament made their complaints against the new system, the experts attempted their own rebuttal, and in this rebuttal we can see the three themes that had first emerged as part of the rhetorical strategy invented by reformers in Chicago.

THE ATTACK ON MOTIVES

The argument that any discretion left to line officials would be used for patronage purposes was asserted repeatedly in 1918–23. Hodgetts et al. have observed that "[o]ne of the dominating features [of the commission's activities in these years] was the tendency to picture the patronage temptation as an almost overwhelming urge which sooner or later took possession of most people in any position to dispense it."[228] Griffenhagen himself seemed to suggest that the commission itself was the only bulwark against the "strongly entrenched spoils system" that had previously dominated the Canadian civil service: "Although many committees and individuals have investigated, reported, criticized, and generalized regarding conditions in the Civil Service of Canada ... it remained to the Commission to settle down to the exacting, tedious, and thankless task of providing the foundations upon which actual improvements could be based."[229] The notion that an "absolutely fair and just" administration was one that strictly limited managerial interference in personnel decisions quickly became pervasive.[230] A pamphlet, which the commission distributed to employees in 1921, proclaimed: "Patronage is dead. Favouritism is as nearly eliminated as human nature and the inexorable process of Departmental procedure will allow. Today, entrance to the Civil Service is by way of competition, and is ruthlessly just."[231] Of course, this must have been galling to the deputy heads, then complaining about the inexorable process of commission procedure.

THE APPEAL TO SCIENCE

Griffenhagen's report on the Canadian civil service was presented in the style and vocabulary of "scientific" work. He prefaced his recommendations with "a theoretical analysis of the personnel problem, as it exists in any large organization." He explained:

> The development of the science of management in the last ten years has done much for clear thinking on administrative problems by standardizing terminology and clarifying concepts. Perhaps we may be pardoned if we introduce this discussion of the Civil Service

employment problem with a brief statement of the distinctions that have come to be generally recognized. ... The term "management" is taken to mean the process of directing and utilizing human skill and effort to secure a desired result. The desired result naturally depends upon the nature of the enterprise. In the case of the Government of Canada, it is to administer the laws of the land in the interests of the people. We may assume that the ideal of the management is the attainment of the maximum efficiency and economy in this process, and we will endeavour in this analysis to set forth specifically ... those practical requirements that must be met if this ideal of administration is to be achieved.

The recommended reforms themselves were then presented as strict imperatives, which were shown to be derived from "well-established principles" of personnel management. Recommendations about methods of appointment were said to be essential for "scientific selection of employees"; recommendations for dismissal were deduced from the "theory of removals"; the recommendations regarding superannuation were commended as part of a "scientific retirement plan."[232]

One of the major entailments of the appeal to science was the notion that all the jurisdictions undergoing reform were of the same class: this had to be true if there were to be general "scientific principles" governing reform. And Griffenhagen did, indeed, make this assertion:

The history of civil service reform has been about the same in all countries. There have been the same deplorable conditions resulting from the patronage system to spur on the advocates of better government, the same active opposition by the beneficiaries of spoils methods, the same right-thinking public opinion effective when aroused but hard to arouse, and the same succession of victories and defeats.[233]

Griffenhagen made the same argument a year later in a report to the U.S. Congress and this time explicitly classed the Chicagoan and Canadian experiences together:

[There has recently] been an important series of classifications beginning with that in the city of Chicago and including those of the State of Illinois, the State of New Jersey, the city of New York, the State of New York, ... and most recently, of the entire civil service of the Dominion of Canada. ... [I]n these classifications and salary standardizations many of the same problems had been encountered. ... [T]hese undertakings [have] resulted in the discovery of certain principles, and the development of certain policies, that are almost universally applicable.[234]

Similarly, the Canadian Civil Service Commission argued in its annual report that "[i]n one form or another the same evils are met with in all services. They are not novel nor peculiar to any jurisdiction, and the methods for correcting them have been developed by long experience ... into a definite science."[235]

A second entailment of the appeal to science was the notion that civil service administration was a subject that could only be properly managed by a person or agency well-trained in appropriate theory. This, too, was a common theme in Griffenhagen's work: audiences were reminded that reform was a "highly specialized line of work" – an "intricate and technical" subject that required the attention of "specialists of proved fitness in the field."[236] Griffenhagen had warned the Canadian government that the classification of the New York City service had been badly flawed and delayed for four years because of the "lack of expertness of personnel" assigned to the job – a claim the Borden government used in Parliament to defend its hiring of Griffenhagen.[237] (This was probably not a fair characterization of the situation in New York City. Its commission had completed the classification in about a year, but political opposition held up implementation for three years. Nevertheless, Griffenhagen liked this argument, using it not only in Ottawa but also in Washington a year later.[238])

THE APPEAL TO CONSENSUS

Griffenhagen and the commission staff also sought to validate their expertise by demonstrating their personal affiliation with the broader expert community and the consistency of their advice with the "accepted wisdom" of the expert community. The commission sought to defend Griffenhagen and his staff by showing that they had "high professional standing in the employment field";[239]

Griffenhagen, in turn, praised Foran as a man "thoroughly conversant with the best modern practice in Civil Service administration."[240]

The experts also sought to demonstrate the value of the reforms themselves through reference to the broader expert community. In June 1919, for example, Griffenhagen argued:

> It may be thought by some that the work being undertaken by the Canadian Civil Service Commission ... [is] in the nature of experiments and out of line with the dictates of experience. This is not so. ... Canada is working along lines that have been found to be the most effective, practical, and representative of the best thought of civil service specialists the world over. ... [T]he measures now under consideration by the Civil Service Commission of Canada will, if adopted, place the Dominion in the vanguard of progressive states with respect to that part of the administration of public business which relates to the civil service.[241]

Some time later, Griffenhagen made a similar defence of the broad powers now enjoyed by the Civil Service Commission. "All progressive countries" had such commissions, Griffenhagen wrote. Furthermore,

> [i]t has been the conclusion of those of my colleagues who have had the closest contact with the public service that without ... a strong and competent civil service commission it is inconceivable that those conditions of democracy, fairness, and opportunity, so essential to an efficient public service, can be expected.[242]

There were also more indirect references to the fact that the reforms Griffenhagen put forward had the imprimatur of "civil service specialists." Griffenhagen assured his audiences that his "Chicago system" had been "accepted as fundamentally right in a large number of jurisdictions"[243] and the commission itself argued that the "investigatorial function," which it proposed to give to its organization branch, "has become generally considered as one of prime importance. The trend of legislation is to recognize ... the advantage of setting up ... a staff to study the service."[244]

Griffenhagen and his staff not only brought a system of personnel administration – the "Chicago Plan" – to Canada, they also brought a way of talking and arguing about personnel administration that shaped the character of debate about civil service reform in the years following 1918. The modes of argument, which I have characterized as the Chicago reformers' "rhetorical strategy," were not entirely alien to Canada; if this were the case, the arguments would have been entirely ineffective. Canada, too, was captured by the possibilities of progress through "science," although perhaps not quite to the extent of its neighbour to the south. There was also a puritanical streak to the rhetoric of some Canadian reformers – particularly those activists whose campaigning for civil service reform was combined with campaigning for temperance – just as there was a heavy dose of moralizing in the language of early Chicagoan reformers.[245] However, we should not put too much emphasis on the similarities between Canadian and Chicagoan reform rhetoric because they are exceeded in magnitude by the differences. It was not common, before 1918, for Canadian reformers to dwell on the iniquities of line officials or to appeal so heavily to the authority of science and the fact of consensus within an expert community; all of these themes gained prominence after 1918 because they were central to the experts' way of defending their reforms. In contemporary terms, we would say that the experts not only put forward a reform but defined the terms in which the debate over that reform would be conducted. Unfortunately, the rhetorical strategy, which had been invented by the Chicago reformers to defend the Chicago Plan and which had been exported to Canada, had three disagreeable effects on the character of the debate over the 1918–19 reforms.

The first was to blind most participants in the debate to the parochial character of the Chicago Plan. In fact, nobody in Canada referred to the new system by that name. Instead, they knew it only as a system whose design was dictated by "science" or recommended by "specialists the world over." The rhetorical strategy invented by the Chicago reformers had the effect of transforming the idiosyncratic aspects of the Chicago Plan into "generally accepted principles." In other words, the experts erased the plan's history, and, as a consequence, it would have been very difficult for a Canadian audience to recognize or argue that the specific circumstances that had influenced the plan did not also hold in Canada. No one, in fact, appears to have made such an argument during the 1918–23 debate.

A second effect of the strategy was to deafen experts to the deputies' complaints against the system. The worldview induced by the rhetorical strategy that had been imported into Canada was to some degree "self-sealing": one could take the complaints themselves as evidence that the commission was doing what it ought to do. The deputies' complaints about the inadequacy of the classification within their individual departments were taken as evidence that the commission was doing a good job of "fulfilling its duty as expressed in the law, namely, that of providing a uniform standard classification as between departments."[246] Similarly, one could discount complaints against the commission's ruthlessness because, after all, one would have anticipated complaints when controls were placed on corrupt line officials. As the Canadian commission explained in 1920, "it was scarcely to be expected that changes which took from departmental heads, as well as from politicians, many of their old-time powers and privileges, and placed them in the hands of the Commission would be invariably accepted without protest or demur. ..."[247] In fact, an expert had to be careful not to be taken in by *any* complaint, no matter how worthy it might at first seem, as a colleague of Griffenhagen's later explained:

> The most vigorous and upright administrators will make common cause with the weakest and most corrupt in denouncing any centralized control ... because, forsooth, who can know so well as the administrator in charge the capabilities of the employees under his direction. To one who does know the service, that sounds convincing, but ... it generally develops that the upper politically selected administrative officers do not know the duties of the employees under their direction.[248]

A third effect of the strategy was to eliminate almost entirely the possibility of compromise with the deputies. An expert could not cede authority to officials if they were not also "specialists" in reform or if one did not believe them likely to exercise discretion properly. Nor could an expert make concessions to suit local conditions if it had already been asserted that all cases were, in all fundamental respects, alike, and that there were general principles about civil service administration that covered all such cases. Similarly, an expert could not make concessions on the design of a reform if those changes would result in a significant deviation from what the expert community had already endorsed or, to put it more concretely, if it deviated substantially from the model law.

The rhetorical strategy that had been employed by Griffenhagen and his staff and the staff of the organization branch constrained them to take a very firm line: if they were to seem sincere in their assertion of these three themes, they were also obliged to take the position that no one should be allowed to lay "unholy hands" on the Civil Service Act. It is conspicuous that the only changes the commission did accept were not modifications of the design of the act, but rather straight exemptions of certain classes from the coverage of the act, which the commission construed not as compromises but rather as a delimitation of its jurisdiction to the "really important" part of the public service.[249]

WHY DID THE EXPERTS PERSIST WITH THIS STRATEGY?

There are at least two reasons why the experts working on civil service reform would have persisted in using this rhetorical strategy even when the inflexible position it demanded seemed likely to get the commission in trouble or even to jeopardize the Civil Service Act itself. The first is that this rhetorical strategy was a means by which the experts could defend themselves against attacks on their standing in debates over civil service reform. By 1920 the experts working on the Canadian reforms had caught themselves in a vicious circle. As controversy over the reforms became more intense, direct challenges to the competence of Griffenhagen and his staff became common. "What firm in Chicago," a member of Parliament asked in June 1919, "would know about the working out of the Civil Service system of Canada?"[250] Another asked "whether a commission of experts composed of our own officials would not have done the work better than this important commission."[251] In the *Ottawa Journal*, a disgruntled public servant wrote:

As to the so-called experts: It would be interesting to know who they are and what qualifications they possess for the work. What experience have they had in this work? Some of them, at least, confessed that this was their first job of this kind. They may be efficiency experts in the conduct of a factory or commercial house, but the Book of Classification bears abundant evidence that they wholly fail to distinguish the difference between these institutions and a Civil Service. The best that can be said of labors, which cost the country upwards of half a million dollars, is that it is an effort to accomplish a difficult task, for the performance of which they were not well qualified, on account of their lack of knowledge of the organization and operation of the Civil Service of Canada, and their false assumption that it can be cast in the mold of a commercial institution.[252]

Indeed, it shortly became the fashion in Ottawa to refer, not merely to the experts who had designed the reforms, but to the "so-called experts" or the "supposed experts." Even Alexander Maclean, minister responsible for the reform legislation in the House of Commons in 1919, succumbed to the unfortunate habit of referring to Griffenhagen and his staff as the "so-called efficiency experts." "'So-called' is the proper word to use!" shouted Sir Sam Hughes, and the House burst with laughter.[253]

At a time when opposition to the new system seemed strong enough to pose a threat to its survival, these challenges to the competence of the experts who had installed it were crucially important. Yet there was no way the experts could substantiate their claim to expertise by appeal to the sorts of reasons traditionally used to substantiate a claim to expertise. In 1912, Sir George Murray had had no difficulty in establishing himself as an "executive expert"; he could fall back on his long experience in the British government and his close association with British high society, an important consideration if one of the objectives of reform was to show fidelity to the "mother country." At the start of his investigation, the *Ottawa Journal* had made a lavish introduction on its front page:

Rt. Hon. Sir George Murray, G.E.B., of London, Eng., well known in financial circles, and an executive expert, who was invited to Canada by Rt. Hon. R.L. Borden, to inquire into Canadian civil service methods, with a view to reform, is in town, and registered at the Chateau Laurier. Sir George is a son of the late Rev. G.E. Murray, rector of Southfleet, Kent. He was educated at Harrow, Christ Church, Oxford, and entered foreign office in 1873. He was transferred to treasury in 1880, appointed private secretary to Rt. Hon. W.E. Gladstone, and Earl of Rosebery, when they were prime minister, chairman Board of Inland Revenue 1897–99, and secretary to the post office 1899–1903.

As regards civil service and financial matters, he is well versed. Last year his services were placed at the disposal of the South African government in regard to the financial relations of provinces to the new union. ... This is his first visit here, and his mission will likely involve a period of about eight weeks, during which time he will make a thorough investigation of all departments of the Canadian civil service, and it is expected that at its conclusion some important changes will be recommended.[254]

Obviously, none of the Chicago reformers could put on a show like this. What, indeed, did Griffenhagen (a thirty-two-year-old civil engineer) or Jacobs (another young engineer) or Telford (a former high school teacher) or Catherwood (a patent lawyer) know about the Canadian or British services? And what experience had they in practical administration, except their two years' experience in reforming the Illinois services? The only way in which these experts could maintain a claim to authority was by attacking the credibility of their critics or by appealing to the idea of a "science" of civil service administration or by appealing to the fact of an expert consensus on the advice they offered. But with the repeated assertion of these claims the possibility of compromise grew even smaller.

Experts within the organization branch, whose own competence in making personnel decisions was aggressively challenged by the deputy ministers, faced a similar predicament. How could a young staff member within the organization branch presume to control the staff of a deputy head who had been in the service for twenty years? It seemed it was only by asserting – as the commission did assert – that "the selection of employees nowadays has become an approved and established science with definite rules and laws."[255]

But once one had asserted that there were "definite rules and laws" and specified what those rules and laws were, one could not bend them without undermining the claim that there was a science and consequently one's own claim to authority over personnel decisions.[256]

There is a second reason why the experts might have persisted in making these arguments. The political community within Canada – the cabinet ministers, members of Parliament, deputy ministers and other public servants who complained about the new act – was not the only, and perhaps not even the most important, audience for these experts. A second audience consisted of American reformers within the National Assembly of Civil Service Commissions, the National Municipal League and the National Civil Service Reform League – an audience that was fighting a very different struggle and one that would have been highly dismayed if Griffenhagen and Jacobs and their staffs had deviated from what had been established, after considerable argument, as "good practice" in civil service administration. The assembly had made its attitude towards such deviations clear in the preface to Catherwood's model law: "The weak spots in civil service administration have usually been produced by unfortunate concessions which are violations of the underlying principles [of civil service administration]. ... We feel, therefore, that ... there should be no substantial departure from the provisions herein set forth."[257]

There is no doubt, furthermore, that American reformers were watching the reform of the Canadian civil service closely. After receiving the contract from the Canadian Civil Service Commission, Griffenhagen was appointed to the National Municipal League's committee on civil service and efficiency.[258] In December 1918, a delegation of municipal reformers from Baltimore visited Ottawa to inspect Griffenhagen's work.[259] In April 1919, Catherwood arranged for Griffenhagen to give an address to the annual meeting of the National Civil Service Reform League on the progress of reform in Canada.[260] (Catherwood also served as the chief delegate for the Chicago and Illinois civil service reform associations at the same meeting.) Another large delegation of reformers and aldermen from Chicago visited Ottawa in October 1919, just as Griffenhagen's reforms were receiving final consideration by Parliament.[261]

The U.S. reform community was one fighting a large number of battles, which were at least roughly comparable to the battle being fought in Chicago. For four years they had argued about the content of a model law and had finally agreed upon a law, and furthermore they had stipulated that there should be no deviation from it. The Canadian reform was the first major reform undertaken since their adoption of the law. For U.S. reformers it would serve as a valuable precedent in their own local struggles. The executive council of the National Civil Service Reform League had quickly seized on the Canadian reforms for this purpose, arguing in its report for 1919 that Canada had adopted a civil service law "which is far superior in many respects to that of the United States." Another senior officer of the league observed after Griffenhagen's 1919 talk that "[w]hat Mr. Griffenhagen said as to the reclassification of the civil service in Canada ... is what will have to be done in the United States if any substantial good is to be accomplished."[262]

7

The Moral of the Story

In 1918–19, the shape of the Canadian civil service changed dramatically and so did the terms in which Canadians thought and argued about problems of civil service administration. In this study I have attempted to show that this dramatic change cannot simply be the result of the interplay of purely domestic social forces, as many recent commentators have been inclined to believe. On the other hand, it is unsatisfactory to lay the fault only on a solitary, incompetent consultant, as early commentators were inclined to do – a sort of managerial equivalent of the "lone gunman" theory. The story is more complicated than that.

The Canadian civil service reforms must be understood in a much larger context, as one of dozens of battles over civil service reform that were being fought in municipal and state governments across the United States. The newly established community of civil service reformers was one whose claim to authority over questions of civil service administration was only tenuously established. Consequently, this community was preoccupied with the task of inventing and disseminating arguments – a rhetorical strategy – that would be effective in persuading a wavering public to support its reform initiatives. The Canadian case became important to this community precisely because of its utility in accomplishing this task. The Canadian commission was invited to join the assembly because of the rhetorical importance of Canadian practice. The reforms of 1918–19 were used by the assembly for rhetorical purposes, and the status of the Canadian commission within the assembly was intimately tied to the fact it had put itself "in the vanguard," as Griffenhagen put it,[263] in the assembly's battle for civil service reform.

Chicago reformers, led by Robert Catherwood, played an important part in shaping the rhetorical strategy that would be used by members of the civil service assembly, and it is consequently not surprising that the strategy should reflect the particular character of the battle over reform in Chicago. The main themes embodied in the strategy – the emphasis on the corruption and incompetence of the opponents of reform, the appeal to science, the demand for conformity to a model law based on Catherwood's "efficiency plan" – all have roots in the Chicago reform experience. These same themes would soon be echoed in many other jurisdictions, including Canada.

Two of the unfortunate weaknesses of this rhetorical strategy were its inability to recognize that battles for reform in different jurisdictions might differ in important respects and its inability to permit compromise or adaptation to local circumstances. In hindsight, we can see that the battle over reform in Ottawa between 1918–23 was one largely precipitated because of the experts' inability to acknowledge or accommodate the unique circumstances of the Canadian case. The result was that the Canadian government retained a system of civil service administration that was, as deputy ministers said at the time, unnecessarily cumbersome. The system of civil service administration established in Ottawa in 1918–19 was a product of turn-of-the-century Chicago politics. It was intended to be an antidote to the chaos and corruption of Chicago's municipal government. In the Canadian federal government, which was neither anarchic nor systemically corrupt, the Chicago Plan was unwieldy and unnecessary.

WHAT CAN WE LEARN FROM THE EXPERIENCE OF 1918–23?

The year 1918 seems like a very long time ago, and we may wonder whether there is much of anything to be learned from the experience of the reforms begun in that year.

As a preface, it is important to remember that, even though the battle with Edwin Griffenhagen might have long since ended, the chief product of the reform exercise – the civil service system itself – lasted in Canada decades afterwards. Parts of the Griffenhagen system remain with us today. It is interesting to speculate, for example, what the Canadian civil service system might have looked like today if a different model – perhaps more like the decentralized system employed by the British civil service – had been adopted in 1918–19.

Griffenhagen's legacy consisted of more than a set of rules about roles and responsibilities in the area of personnel management. It also consisted of a way of thinking and arguing about personnel management and of justifying the system put in place in 1918–19. The bundle of arguments imported by Griffenhagen was adopted by the Civil Service Commission, and then by other defenders of the new system, and continued in use long after Griffenhagen himself had been forgotten. Key assumptions that might at first have seemed highly contentious, such as those about the condition of the public service before the 1918–19 reforms or about the trustworthiness of line managers in making personnel decisions, were gradually taken to be axiomatic. Edwin Griffenhagen helped to change the way we talked about the civil service. In this sense, the effects of the 1918–19 reforms could be seen in the 1991 debate over the Public Service Reform Act, which I discussed in the first chapter.

One of the important purposes served by a closer review of the 1918–19 reforms is to remind us that many of these axioms are at least contestable and perhaps even flat wrong. "We all know the history of the public service," said one critic during the 1991 debates. Do we really? It is arguable that some of the things we think we know from historical experience are not, in fact, the products of *our* history at all, but rather that of the City of Chicago. This is not to say that concerns about reforms such as those embodied in the 1991 Public Service Reform Act are unjustified. Rather, it is only to suggest that those concerns may have to be justified on grounds other than an appeal to history.

The experience of 1918–23 also provides us with a cautionary lesson about our attempts to model public service reforms on those of other countries. Of course, it would be foolish to suggest that we should ignore the experience of other public services or overlook innovative practices that may well produce benefits at home. On the other hand, it is important to remember that public services are not interchangeable: each is shaped by distinctive political and social conditions and is the product of a unique series of historical events. We would be well advised, when looking over our borders for models for reform, to question whether those models were designed to accommodate circumstances very different from our own. Canadian officials did not do this in 1918, either because of the pressure to complete reforms quickly or because they were flattered to imagine themselves as the leaders of a continent-wide movement for public service reform. It is not difficult to imagine that we might be tempted to make a similar mistake today.

There is also a related lesson to be learned about the relationship between governmental decision makers and people like Edwin Griffenhagen who claim to be experts in one field or another. When I say that people sometimes claim to be experts I do mean to imply that the claim of expertise they put forward is necessarily untenable. (In Edwin Griffenhagen's case, however, we might well have cause to wonder about its reasonableness.) What I mean to imply is only that an individual's expertise is never self-evident. A claim of expertise must somehow be put forward and substantiated. Often this claim must be made to audiences who are, at the start, sceptical about the individual's expertise. A substantial amount of effort may then be invested in the project of demonstrating one's own qualifications.

None of this is news to individuals in the consulting business who know that their advice is often coolly received. One practitioner observes that clients often regard management consultants with "mistrust and suspicion,"[264] while another says that clients often regard consultants as "scrounging and interfering charlatans" who exaggerate their own competence and prey on the insecurities of their clientele.[265] This credibility problem is sometimes so severe, a third author argues, that the consultant's major challenge is often to "convince the client – without appearing to do so – that you are loyal, trustworthy, and responsible, [and] good at what you do. Here, you are working against long-established prejudices against consultants in general."[266]

Experts spend a substantial amount of time inventing techniques to respond to these "long-established prejudices." They develop arguments about their competence and trustworthiness and about the reasonableness of their advice. They also develop ways of working that reinforce those arguments; that is, they try to act in such a way as to convince you of their expertise.[267] Experts rarely do this independently. More often, members of an expert community – a group of individuals claiming to specialize in the same field – collaborate in the development of persuasive arguments and ways of working. The process of developing these arguments and routines is one of *bricolage* in which ideas already current in popular culture are adopted and shaped to suit the expert community. To take a prosaic example; the appeal to consensus within an expert community – a very common way of establishing the reasonableness of an individual expert's advice[268] – plays on the common-sense notion that a proposition widely agreed upon is less likely to be egregiously wrong. Similarly, another popular method of justifying advice – the appeal to "academic theory and scientific advice"[269] – would not work in a society that did not already think highly of the sciences and scientific knowledge.

Experts who rely on arguments such as these to establish their expertise are also bound by them. This is an important point that is not always appreciated by academics who study the professions. While many academics recognize that expert communities are heavily engaged in the task of justifying their authority, there is a common tendency to regard the arguments and routines developed for this purpose as mere façades behind which the experts are free to do what they want. In practice, however, this is anything but the case. Experts cannot say one thing and do another. They must act in a way consistent with the arguments put forward to justify their claims to expertise. If an expert insists that there is consensus within an expert community about the right solution to a problem or says that there is a body of scientific knowledge about a certain problem, then the expert cannot deviate from that consensus or that body of scientific knowledge in a particular case. The inconsistency is bound to be noticed. Denigration of local knowledge and downplaying of the peculiarities of a specific case are unintended but necessary consequences of the expert community's attempt to establish its authority.

If the specific case does not deviate much from the average case, then the expert's predicament is not likely to generate much of a problem. If the specific case is distinctive, however, the expert's predicament might become highly problematic. This is probably what happened in 1918–23. If circumstances in Ottawa had been more like those in Chicago, then it might not have mattered as much that Edwin Griffenhagen insisted on installing a system like that recommended by the Assembly of Civil Service Commissions. Of course, circumstances in Ottawa were very different from those in Chicago, and the tendency to deny the significance of local peculiarities and to attack the *bona fides* of individuals who held local knowledge did substantial harm. We might imagine that similar harm might be done to clients of other expert communities that seek to justify their claim to expertise in similar ways. (There are, of course, other reasons why experts might provide clients with bad advice. Some experts, particularly in weakly institutionalized fields, are simply incompetent. Furthermore, advice-giving is often a business, and it might simply be uneconomical for experts to do the extra work necessary for general advice to be tailored to suit an unusual case.)

What lessons then should the consumers of expert advice take from the experience of 1918–23? One lesson might be to understand the preoccupations of the expert community and the character of the problems they typically address and then to consider whether one's own circumstances differ markedly from those typically encountered by members of that expert community. Another lesson is to appreciate how expert communities and their individual members attempt to rationalize their authority and to anticipate how the strategies used for that purpose might constrain the sorts of advice that can be provided in particular cases.

A common injunction to the consumers of expert advice is this: Get a second opinion. The injunction seems sensible, but it has an important limitation. The second expert may be a member of the same expert community as the first expert and may consequently be constrained by the same rhetorical problems. The public servants who believed in July 1919 that their own expert, Louis Jacobs, would serve as an effective check on Edwin Griffenhagen were quite mistaken.[270] The best that Jacobs – a young consultant who travelled in the same circles and relied on the same rhetorical strategies as Griffenhagen – could do was to confirm that Griffenhagen was correctly reporting the conventional wisdom within the Assembly of Civil Service Commissions. The more important question – whether the conventional wisdom suited the Canadian case – went unanswered.

EPILOGUE

Griffenhagen's career enjoyed a substantial boost after his visit to Canada. He had not had a single contract of importance with any government before the Canadian Civil Service Commission hired him in March 1918. By the time he left Ottawa, however, Griffenhagen had been commissioned to reform civil services for the cities of Baltimore, Montreal and Philadelphia and for the state governments of Georgia, Kentucky, Maryland and South Carolina.[271] In the spring of 1919, the U.S. government selected Griffenhagen as chief counsellor to a commission Congress had established to classify the executive departments of the federal government. The U.S. classification, completed by Griffenhagen in 1920, was in fact very much like the one completed in Canada a year earlier. The revised classification plan released in Canada in the fall of 1919 had 1,729 classifications; the U.S. plan had 1,762. Griffenhagen boasted that the Reclassification Act adopted by Congress in 1923 "closely followed" his own draft.[272]

The debate among Canadian academics and public officials about the virtues of the 1918–19 reforms continued for years after the installation of the reforms themselves, but so, too, did the influence of the Chicago reformers. In 1929, for example, the political scientist R. MacGregor Dawson made a severe attack on the reforms in his book, *The Civil Service of Canada*, and criticized the Borden ministry for mishandling the reforms. Borden, then in retirement, was stung by the criticisms. Privately, he complained of Dawson's "pontifical tone in enunciating opinions upon questions of which he has the merest smattering of knowledge."[273] In 1931, Borden published a defence of the reforms. "The Civil Service Act of 1918 was a tremendous step in advance," he wrote, "a very competent judge who for many years was President of the National Civil Service Reform League of the United States has described it as the most advanced measure of civil service reform that any country has adopted."[274]

For some observers these words from the former prime minister may have seemed to settle matters. But few would have known that the "very competent judge" upon whom Borden relied was Robert Catherwood, now also retired, who in 1930 had taken up correspondence with Borden. On Christmas Day 1930, Catherwood wrote to Borden to compliment him on his recently published Oxford lectures:

> I feel that these two books are a truly great contribution to the study of Canadian history. Yet in my humble opinion they are transcended in importance by the Canada Civil Service Act. ... Canada was the first among nations to declare that it is *merit tenure* (in respect to classification, pay, promotions, career, etc. as well as selection) upon which efficency depends. We are copying the idea in the States, but ... have not as yet improved upon the Canadian expression of the principle.[275]

Some time later, Catherwood wrote again to Borden:

> Now in Canada you have a fine civil service law. I know Dr. Adam Short [sic], C.M.G., the Hon. Dr. Roche, Col. La Rochelle [sic] K.C., and Mr. Jamieson [sic] (deceased) ... and as delightful gentlemen and pleasant companions, they rank with the non-entities on the Washington Commission. ... Eminent in other directions but of no use on administrative matters. I should say that none of them was quite up to the Act of 1918. Would the Bell Telephone Co. and the Sun Life Assurance Co. engage any of them to select its personnel [?][276]

In March 1931, Catherwood wrote to Borden asking if he would accept the position of vice-president of the National Civil Service Reform League, adding that "[t]he Canada civil service act of 1918, passed under your government, was undoubtedly a very great achievement and it is well known that, but for your determined and skillful support both in Parliament and before the country, the bill would not have become law.[277] Borden, still bitter about Dawson's attack, replied, "I am delighted to accept ... [and] please accept my very warm appreciation of your very kind words with respect to my part in civil service reform in Canada."[278]

Notes

1 The two laws were the Civil Service Act, 1918, which came into force on 24 May 1918, and the Civil Service Amendment Act, which came into force on 10 November 1919.

2 Sir Joseph Pope, *Memoirs of a Public Servant* (Toronto: Oxford University Press, 1960), p. 288.

3 Adam Shortt to William Grant, [letter] 16 March 1923 (Ottawa: National Archives of Canada, William Grant Papers, vol. 9, Correspondence Files).

4 Major changes included a shift in authority over classification and salary from the Civil Service Commission (now the Public Service Commission) to the Treasury Board in the 1930s, the introduction of collective bargaining arrangements under the Public Service Staff Relations Act and the introduction of a somewhat more flexible classification system in the 1960s.

5 Canada, Royal Commission on Technical and Professional Services (Beatty Commission), *Report* (Ottawa: King's Printer, 1930), pp. 16–18.

6 Canada, Royal Commission on Administrative Classifications in the Public Service (Gordon Commission), *Report of the Royal Commission* (Ottawa: King's Printer, 1946), pp. 13–14.

7 Canada, Royal Commission on Government Organization (Glassco Commission), *Management of the Public Service* (Ottawa: Queen's Printer, 1962), pp. 44 and 50.

8 Canada, Royal Commission on Financial Management and Accountability (Lambert Commission), *Final Report* (Ottawa: Supply and Services Canada, 1979), p. 115.

9 Canada, Public Service 2000, *The Renewal of the Public Service of Canada: Synopsis* (Ottawa: Supply and Services Canada, 1990), pp. 4 and 14 and *Report of the Task Force on Staffing* (Ottawa: Privy Council Office, 1990), p. 4.

10 Bill C-26 was given first reading on 18 June 1991 and received royal assent on December 17, 1992 (40–41 Elizabeth II, c.54).

11 Canada, House of Commons, Legislative Committee on Bill C-26, *Minutes and Proceedings*. 34th Parliament, 3rd Session, no. 1, 9 March 1992 (Ottawa: Supply and Services Canada, 1992), pp. 26–7.

12 Lambert Commission, *Final Report*, p. 112.
13 Taylor Cole, *The Canadian Bureaucracy* (Durham, N.C.: Duke University Press, 1949), p. 35.
14 Glassco Commission, *Management of the Public Service*, p. 42.
15 Public Service 2000, *Renewal of the Public Service of Canada: Synopsis*, p. 2.
16 Legislative Committee on Bill C-26, *Minutes and Proceedings*. 34th Parliament, 3rd Session, no. 10, 31 March 1992, p. 30; Canada, House of Commons, *Debates*. 34th Parliament, 3rd Session, vol. 5, 10 February 1992 (Ottawa: Supply and Services Canada, 1992), p. 6692.
17 Legislative Committee on Bill C-26, *Minutes and Proceedings*. 34th Parliament, 3rd Session, no. 7, 24 March 1992, p. 11.
18 *Debates*. 34th Parliament, 3rd Session, vol. 10, 17 June 1992, p. 12317.
19 See also *Debates*. 34th Parliament, 3rd Session, vol. 6, 21 February 1992, p. 7458; and *Debates*. 34th Parliament, 3rd Session, vol. 10, 23 June 1992, p. 12690.
20 *Debates*. 34th Parliament, 3rd Session, vol. 6, 11 February 1992, p. 6781.
21 For other instances in which this claim was made, see Legislative Committee on Bill C-26, *Minutes and Proceedings*. 34th Parliament, 3rd Session, no. 13, 2 April 1992, p. 41–2; *Debates*. 34th Parliament, 3rd Session, vol. 5, 10 February 1992, pp. 6636–7; vol. 6, 11 February 1992, p. 6783; vol. 10, 17 June 1992, p. 12315.
22 Shortt to Grant, [letter] 16 March 1923 [emphasis in the original]. The letter may overstate Shortt's antipathy towards "things American." He was a founding member of the American Political Science Association and was its vice-president in 1913.
23 William L. Grant, "The Civil Service of Canada," *The University of Toronto Quarterly* 3:4 (July 1934), p. 435.
24 R. McGregor Dawson, "The Canadian Civil Service," *Canadian Journal of Economics and Political Science* 2:3 (August 1936), p. 292.
25 Memorial of the Civil Service Association of Ottawa to the Rt. Hon. Arthur Meighen, 16 August 1921 (Ottawa: National Archives of Canada, Arthur Meighen Papers, vol. 19), p. 10719.
26 Alasdair Roberts, "The Rhetorical Problems of the Management Expert" (Ph.D. diss., Harvard University, 1994).
27 See Alasdair Roberts, "Demonstrating Neutrality: The Rockefeller Philanthropies and the Evolution of Public Administration, 1927–1936," *Public Administration Review* 54:3 (May/June 1994), pp. 221–8; "Why the Brownlow Committee Failed: Neutrality and Partisanship in the Early Years of Public Administration," forthcoming in *Administration and Society*; "The Brownlow–Brookings Feud: The Politics of Dissent Within the Academic Community," *Journal of Policy History* 7:3 (Summer 1995).
28 Alasdair Roberts, "'Civic Discovery' as a Rhetorical Strategy," *Journal of Policy Analysis and Management* 14:2 (Spring 1995), pp. 291–307.
29 See, for example, James G. March and Johan P. Olsen, *Rediscovering Institutions* (New York: Free Press, 1989), pp. 69–94; Christopher Hood and Michael Jackson, *Administrative Argument* (London: Gower, 1991); Christopher Hood and Michael Jackson, "Keys for Locks in Administrative Argument," *Administration and Society* 25:4 (February 1994), pp. 467–88.

30 Charles E. Merriam, *Chicago* (New York: Macmillan, 1929), p. 90.

31 Joseph B. Kingsbury, "The Merit System in Chicago from 1895 to 1915, Part 4," *Public Personnel Studies* 4:6 (June 1926), p. 179.

32 Clifford W. Patton, *The Battle for Municipal Reform* (College Park, Md.: McGrath Publishing Company, 1940), p. 40.

33 Lloyd Wendt and H. Kogan, *Bosses in Lusty Chicago* (Bloomington, Ind.: Indiana University Press, 1974), p. 36.

34 Charles Beard, "Chicago Treasurers to Face Charge," *National Municipal Review* 1:1 (1912), p. 157.

35 See, generally, Samuel Hays, "The Politics of Reform in Municipal Government in the Progressive Era," in Blaine Brownell and W. Stickle, eds., *Bosses and Reformers: Urban Politics in America, 1880–1920* (Boston: Houghton Mifflin Company, 1973); Richard Hofstadter, *The Age of Reform* (New York: Vintage Books, 1955); James Weinstein, *The Corporate Ideal in the Liberal State* (Boston: Beacon Press, 1968); Robert Wiebe, *Businessmen and Reform: A Study of the Progressive Movement* (Cambridge: Harvard University Press, 1962).

36 Hofstadter, *Age of Reform*, p. 186.

37 Ibid., pp. 202–3, 319–22.

38 Douglas Sutherland, *Fifty Years on the Civic Front* (Chicago: Civic Federation, 1943), p. 27.

39 Michael P. McCarthy, "Businessmen and Professionals in Municipal Reform: The Chicago Experience, 1887–1920" (Ph.D. diss., Northwestern University, 1970), p. 42; Charles E. Merriam, "Investigations as a Means of Securing Administrative Efficiency," *Annals* 41 (1912), pp. 281–303.

40 C.R. Atkinson, "Recent Graft Exposures and Prosecutions," *National Municipal Review*, 1:4 (October 1912), p. 678.

41 Maureen Flanagan, *Charter Reform in Chicago* (Carbondale, Ill.: Southern Illinois University Press, 1987), p. 40.

42 Patton, *Battle for Municipal Reform*, p. 49.

43 Ibid., p. 45.

44 T.H. Watkins, *Righteous Pilgrim: The Life and Times of Harold L. Ickes* (New York: Henry Holt and Company, 1990), pp. 60–1 and 94.

45 Maureen Flanagan, "Fred A. Busse: A Silent Mayor in Turbulent Times," in Paul Green and M.G. Holli, eds., *The Mayors: The Chicago Political Tradition* (Carbondale, Ill.: Southern Illinois University Press, 1987).

46 Ibid.

47 See McCarthy, "Businessmen and Professionals in Municipal Reform" (Ph.D. diss.), pp. 142 and 209.

48 Robert C. Catherwood, "Efficiency in the Public Service of Chicago," in National Civil Service Reform League, *Proceedings of the Twenty-Eighth Annual Meeting* (Chicago: National Civil Service Reform League, 1909); "The Development of Efficiency in the Civil Service," in National Civil Service Reform League, *Proceedings of the Twenty-Ninth Annual Meeting* (Chicago: National Civil Service Reform League, 1910), pp. 163–75.

49 Watkins, *Righteous Pilgrim*, p. 106; Merriam, "Investigations as a Means of Securing Administrative Efficiency," *Annals*.

50 Kingsbury, "Merit System in Chicago," *Public Personnel Studies* 4:6, p. 180.

51 Merriam, "Investigations as a Means of Securing Administrative Efficiency," *Annals*, pp. 298 and 301; Kingsbury, "Merit System in Chicago," *Public Personnel Studies*, p. 180; Chicago, Civil Service Commission, *Fourteenth Annual Report* (Chicago: Civil Service Commission, 1909), pp. 10–11.

52 In 1934, Louis Brownlow, head of the Public Administration Clearing House and chair of the Social Science Research Council's Advisory Committee on Public Administration, wrote that Griffenhagen had "more experience in [the field of Public Administration] than anybody else in the United States ... [and] the largest library and the most valuable collection of material extant." Louis Brownlow, [diary] 31 December 1934 (Boston, Mass.: John F. Kennedy Library Archives, Louis Brownlow Papers, Box 43). Griffenhagen was a charter member of the Association of Consulting Management Engineers and its president in 1948. His firm continued to operate internationally until the mid-1970s, when it was incorporated into the John Diebold Group of New York. Griffenhagen died in Quincy, Illinois, in 1982. Author's correspondence with Mr. John Diebold, January 1990; *The New York Times*, 11 February 1982, p. B5.

53 Albert N. Marquis, ed., *Who's Who in America, 1926–1927* (Chicago: A.N. Marquis Company, 1927), p. 842; Glen A. Bishop, ed., *Chicago's Accomplishments and Leaders* (Chicago: Bishop Publishing, 1933), p. 227.

54 Kingsbury, "Merit System in Chicago," *Public Personnel Studies* 4:6, p. 183.

55 Catherwood, "Development of Efficiency in the Civil Service," in National Civil Service Reform League, *Proceedings of the Twenty-Ninth Annual Meeting*, p. 172.

56 Chicago, Civil Service Commission, *Seventeenth Annual Report* (Chicago: Civil Service Commission, 1912), p. 14.

57 Merriam, "Investigations as a Means of Securing Administrative Efficiency," *Annals*, p. 297.

58 Chicago, Civil Service Commission, *Eighteenth Annual Report* (Chicago: Civil Service Commission, 1913), p. 12.

59 James Miles, "Municipal Efficiency: What Is It?" in National Assembly of Civil Service Commissions, *Proceedings of the Fifth Annual Meeting* (New York: Chief Publishing Company, 1912), p. 57.

60 Richard Lindberg, *To Serve and Collect: Chicago Politics and Police Corruption* (New York: Praeger, 1991), p. 108; Lloyd Wendt and H. Kogan, *Lords of the Levee* (Indianapolis, Ind.: Bobbs-Merrill Company, 1943), p. 295.

61 Robert Catherwood, "The Investigation of Chicago's Police," *National Municipal Review* 1:2 (April 1912), pp. 289–91.

62 Robert Catherwood, "The Future of the Merit System," in National Assembly of Civil Service Commissions, *Proceedings of the Eighth Annual Meeting* (New York: Chief Publishing Company, 1915), p. 70.

63 Samuel Dauchy, "Report on the Illinois Civil Service Commissions," in National Civil Service Reform League, *Proceedings of the Thirty-Second Annual Meeting* (Chicago: National Civil Service Reform League, 1913), p. 32; Edwin O. Griffenhagen, "The Origin of the Modern Occupational Classification in Personnel Administration," *Public Personnel Studies* 2:6 (September 1924),

p. 186; Lewis Meriam, "The Uses of a Personnel Classification in the Public Service," *Annals* 113 (1924), pp. 216 and 219.

64 Louis L. Jacobs, "Standardizing Efficiency in Chicago," in National Assembly of Civil Service Commissions, *Proceedings of the Sixth Annual Meeting* (New York: Chief Publishing Company, 1913), p. 52.

65 National Assembly of Civil Service Commissions, *Proceedings of the Fifth Annual Meeting* (New York: Chief Publishing Company, 1912), p. 67.

66 Robert C. Catherwood, "Widening of the Area of the Functions of Civil Service Commissions," in National Assembly of Civil Service Commissions, *Proceedings of the Sixth Annual Meeting* (New York: Chief Publishing Company, 1913), p. 118.

67 Elton Lower, "Movement for Efficiency," in National Assembly of Civil Service Commissions, *Proceedings of the Fourth Meeting* (New York: Chief Publishing Company, 1911), p. 47.

68 Griffenhagen, "Origin of the Modern Occupational Classification," *Public Personnel Studies*, p. 193.

69 National Assembly of Civil Service Commissions, *Proceedings of the Fourth Annual Meeting* (New York: Chief Publishing Company, 1911), p. 16.

70 Merriam, *Chicago*, p. 225.

71 Patton, *Battle for Municipal Reform*, p. 3.

72 Hays, "Politics of Reform in Municipal Government," in Brownell and Stickle, *Bosses and Reformers*, pp. 138–9.

73 See Blain Brownell and W. Stickle, *Bosses and Reformers: Urban Politics in America, 1880–1920* (Boston: Houghton Mifflin Company, 1973), pp. 163–7.

74 See, for example, Catherwood, "Development of Efficiency in the Civil Service," in National Civil Service Reform League, *Proceedings of the Twenty-Ninth Annual Meeting*, p. 163.

75 Ari Hoogenboom, *Outlawing the Spoils* (Urbana, Ill.: University of Illinois Press, 1961), p. 251.

76 Patton, *Battle for Municipal Reform*, p. 32.

77 National Assembly of Civil Service Commissions, *Proceedings of the Ninth Annual Meeting* (Ottawa: King's Printer, 1916), p. 127.

78 See Frank B. Gilbreth, *Primer of Scientific Management* (New York: Van Nostrand Company, 1912).

79 Catherwood, "Development of Efficiency in the Civil Service," in National Civil Service Reform League, *Proceedings of the Twenty-Ninth Annual Meeting*, p. 165.

80 Catherwood, "Functions of Civil Service Commissions," in National Assembly of Civil Service Commissions, *Proceedings of the Sixth Annual Meeting*, pp. 115–16.

81 Griffenhagen, "Origin of the Modern Occupational Classification," *Public Personnel Studies*, p. 184.

82 Edwin O. Griffenhagen, "The Principle and Technique of Preparing an Occupational Classification of Positions in the Public Service," *Public Personnel Studies* 2:8 (November 1924), pp. 240–53.

83 See J. Louis Jacobs, *Review of Movement for Standardization of Public Employ-ments* (Chicago: J.L. Jacobs Company, 1916).

84 See New York Bureau of Municipal Research, "Standardization of Public Employments, Part I," *Municipal Research* 67 (November 1915), pp. 23–4; William C. Beyer, "Standardization of Salaries in American Cities," *National Municipal Review* 5:2 (April 1916), p. 269.

85 Albert S. Faught, "A Review of the Civil Service Laws of the United States," *National Municipal Review* 3:2 (April 1914), p. 318.

86 National Assembly of Civil Service Commissions, *Proceedings of the Fifth Annual Meeting*, p. 60.

87 Robert C. Catherwood, "A Model Civil Service Law," in National Assembly of Civil Service Commissions, *Proceedings of the Eighth Annual Meeting* (New York: Chief Publishing Company, 1915), p. 111.

88 Robert C. Catherwood, "Essential Principles of a Model Civil Service Law for States, Counties, and Cities," in National Assembly of Civil Service Commissions, *Proceedings of the Seventh Annual Meeting* (New York: Chief Publishing Company, 1914), p. 23.

89 W.D. Foulke, *Fighting the Spoilsman* (New York: G.P. Putnam's Sons, 1919), p. 223.

90 Albert S. Faught, "Mr. Catherwood's Draft of a Model Civil Service Law," *National Municipal Review* 3:2 (April 1914), p. 377.

91 Catherwood, "Model Civil Service Law," in National Assembly of Civil Service Commissions, *Proceedings of the Eighth Annual Meeting*.

92 J.E. Campbell, "Powers Which Should Be Exercised By A Civil Service Commission," in National Assembly of Civil Service Commissions, *Proceedings of the Seventh Annual Meeting* (New York: Chief Publishing Company, 1914), p. 38.

93 Catherwood, "Model Civil Service Law," in National Assembly of Civil Service Commissions, *Proceedings of the Eighth Annual Meeting*. p. 14.

94 Nelson Spencer, "New York City's Civil Service," *National Municipal Review* 5:1 (January 1916), pp. 47–55.

95 Clinton Rogers Woodruff, "Other Attacks on the Civil Service," *National Municipal Review* 5:2 (April 1916), p. 379.

96 Frederick Rex, "Analysis of Measures Relating to Municipal Administration and Legislation Submitted to Popular Vote at the November Election," *National Municipal Review* 6:3 (May 1917), p. 389.

97 Griffenhagen, "Origin of the Modern Occupational Classification," *Public Personnel Studies*, p. 193.

98 Jon C. Teaford, *The Twentieth-Century American City*, 2nd edition (Baltimore: Johns Hopkins University Press, 1993), pp. 49–50.

99 Kingsbury, "Merit System in Chicago," *Public Personnel Studies* 4:6.

100 Merriam, *Chicago*, p. 22.

101 McCarthy, "Businessmen and Professionals in Municipal Reform" (Ph.D. diss.), p. 189.

102 Kingsbury, "Merit System in Chicago," *Public Personnel Studies* 4:11, p. 308.

103 Lloyd Wendt and H. Kogan, *Big Bill of Chicago* (Indianapolis, Ind., Bobbs-Merrill Company, 1953), pp. 141–2.

104 National Assembly of Civil Service Commissions, *Proceedings of the Ninth Annual Meeting*, pp. 98–9.

105 Ibid., p. 83.

106 Ibid., pp. 88–9 and 92.

107 Ibid., p. 101.

108 Ibid., pp. 111–12.

109 Ibid., pp. 97–8.

110 Ibid., p. 103.

111 "Mr. William Foran Has Been Elected to the Presidency C.S. Commissions," *Ottawa Journal*, 16 June 1916, p. 11.

112 Canada, Royal Commission on Civil Service (McInnes Commission), *Report of the Commissioners*, Can. Sess. Pap. 44 Victoria (1881), no. 113; Canada, Royal Commission on Civil Service (Hague Commission), *Report of the Commissioners*, Can. Sess. Pap. 55 Victoria (1892), no. 16c; Canada, Royal Commission on Civil Service (Courtney Commission), *Report of the Commissioners*, Can. Sess. Pap. 7 Edward VII (1907), no. 29a.

113 Sir Robert Borden, *Memoirs* (New York: Macmillan, 1938), p. 980.

114 Hague Commission, *Report of the Commissioners*, p. xx.

115 McInnes Commission, *Report of the Commissioners*, pp. 19–20.

116 The best summary of the development of the British service is probably found in the fourth report of the 1914 Macdonnell Commission: United Kingdom, Royal Commission on the Civil Service (Macdonnell Commission), *Fourth Report*, Parliamentary Papers, 1914, Volume XVI, Cd. 7338.

117 Canada, *Statutes of Canada*, Civil Service Amendment Act, 1908, 7–8 Edward VII, c.15.

118 Adam Shortt to Beth Shortt, [letter] 15 September 1908, (Kingston: Queen's University Archives, Adam Shortt Papers, Correspondence Files).

119 Andrew Haydon, "Adam Shortt," *Queen's Quarterly* 38 (Autumn 1931), p. 619. The Indian service had served as a model for reform of the British civil service, and the highest civil service examinations determined appointments to both the higher division of the British civil service and the Indian civil service.

120 Canada, Civil Service Commission, *First Annual Report*, Can. Sess. Pap. 9–10 Edward VII (1910), no. 31.

121 Canada, Civil Service Commission, *Examination Papers, 1913–14*, Can. Sess. Pap. 5 George V (1915), no. 31, p. 110.

122 Adam Shortt to Mr. Chipman, [letter] 14 March 1918 (Kingston: Queen's University Archives, Adam Shortt Papers, Correspondence Files).

123 Adam Shortt to G.A. Warburton, [letter] 4 January 1918 (Kingston: Queen's University Archives, Adam Shortt Papers, Correspondence Files).

124 Sir Joseph Pope, "The Federal Government," in A. Shortt and A.G. Doughty, eds., *Canada and Its Provinces*, vol. 6 (Toronto: Glasgow, Brooks, and Company, 1914) p. 354.

125 James R. Mallory, *The Structure of Canadian Government* (Toronto: Macmillan, 1970), p. 153.

126 See the biographies provided in Parliamentary Press Gallery, *Canadian Parliamentary Guide, 1918* (Ottawa: Mortimer Publishing, 1918), pp. 521–30.

127 Pope, *Memoirs of a Public Servant*, p. 113; John Lewis, "The Laurier Regime, 1896–1911," in A. Shortt and A.G. Doughty, eds., *Canada and Its Province*, vol. 6 (Toronto: Glasgow, Brooks, and Company, 1914), pp. 163–4.

128 Sir Robert Borden, *Problems of an Efficient Civil Service* (Ottawa: King's Printer, 1931), p. 6. The Conservatives' platform in the 1907 election had called for "a thorough and complete reformation of the laws relating to the Civil Service." See J.C. Hopkins, *Canadian Annual Review, 1907* (Toronto: Annual Review Publishing Company, 1908), pp. 459–60.

129 Borden, *Memoirs*, p. 347.

130 Sir George Murray, *Report on the Organization of the Public Service of Canada*, Can. Sess. Pap. 3 George V (1912), no. 57a.

131 Bill 217 was given first reading on 29 May 1914.

132 Sir Robert Borden to Sir George Perley, [letter] 29 November 1930 (Ottawa: National Archives of Canada, Sir Robert Borden Papers, vol. 265), pp. 148567–8. Reform efforts were also hampered by the illness of Thomas White, his minister of finance.

133 Murray, *Organization of the Public Service*.

134 R. McGregor Dawson, *The Civil Service of Canada* (London: Humphrey Milford, 1929), pp. 68–70 and 81; Canada, Civil Service Commission, *Report of the Commissioners, 1914–15*, Can. Sess. Pap. 6 George V (1916), no. 31.

135 William Foran, "The Civil Service Law in Canada," in National Assembly of Civil Service Commissions, *Proceedings of the Eighth Annual Meeting* (New York: Chief Publishing Company, 1915), p. 18.

136 Pope, "Federal Government," in Shortt and Doughty, *Canada and Its Provinces*, p. 362.

137 William Foran, Personnel File (Ottawa: National Archives of Canada, Record Group 32, vol. 93).

138 "William Foran: Great Public Servant," *Ottawa Journal*, 16 January 1939, p. 6.

139 See the correspondence between Foran and Henry T. Ross of the Department of Finance, July 1915, in Foran's personnel file. Foran complained to the secretary of the Treasury Board that other deputies had had similar expenses reimbursed. He eventually got his money.

140 National Assembly of Civil Service Commissions, *Proceedings of the Eighth Annual Meeting* (New York: Chief Publishing Company, 1915), p. 11.

141 National Assembly of Civil Service Commissions, *Proceedings of the Ninth Annual Meeting*, pp. 32–4 and 95.

142 Ibid., p. 34.

143 "Mr. William Foran Has Been Elected to the Presidency C.S. Commissions," *Ottawa Journal*, 16 June 1916, p. 11.

144 "Experts From the C.S. Commissions Gather In Ottawa," *Ottawa Journal*, 14 June 1916, p. 1; "A Superannuation Plan Is Talked Of To-Day By The C.S.

Commissioners," *Ottawa Journal*, 15 June 1916, p. 1; "Mr. William Foran Has Been Elected To The Presidency C.S. Commissions," *Ottawa Journal*, 16 June 1916, p. 11; National Assembly of Civil Service Commissions, *Proceedings of the Ninth Annual Meeting*, p. 173.

145 The text of the October Manifesto can be found in J.C. Hopkins, *Canadian Annual Review, 1917* (Toronto: Annual Review Publishing Company, 1918), pp. 587–90.

146 Sir George Foster, [diary] 8 October to 2 November 1917 (Ottawa: National Archives of Canada, Sir George Foster Papers, vol. 6).

147 Sir Robert Borden to William Roche, [letter] 11 October 1917 (Ottawa: National Archives of Canada, Sir Robert Borden Papers, vol. 87), p. 44570.

148 Clarence Jameson, "Memorandum for Sir Robert Borden," 2 November 1917 (Ottawa: National Archives of Canada, Sir Robert Borden Papers, vol. 87), pp. 44577–88.

149 Foster, [diary] 23 January 1918.

150 Ibid., 24 February 1918.

151 G.A. Warburton to Sir Robert Borden, [letter] 18 January 1918 (Ottawa: National Archives of Canada, Sir Robert Borden Papers, vol. 87), p. 44591.

152 See Alexander Maclean in Canada, House of Commons, *Debates*. 13th Parliament, 1st Session, vol. 1, 12 April 1918 (Ottawa: King's Printer, 1918), p. 695; Sir Robert Borden in *Debates*. 13th Parliament, 1st Session, vol. 1, 19 March 1918, p. 30–1. Order-In-Council, P.C. 358, 13 February 1918: The first draft of this regulation was given to cabinet on 25 January; a second draft was adopted as P.C. 273 on 31 January but was never published. See Sir Robert Borden Papers, vol. 87, pp. 44594–7 and 44603–06.

153 Michel LaRochelle, who had been appointed as a commissioner with Adam Shortt in 1908, continued on after 1917. He does not appear, however, to have been an active member of the commission. Shortt's resignation from the commission was voluntary. His reasons for wanting to leave are laid out in a letter: Adam Shortt to E.R. Peacock, [letter] 19 January 1918 (Kingston: Queen's University Archives, Adam Shortt Papers, Correspondence Files).

154 Before the Special Committee on the Civil Service of Canada (Malcolm Committee), commissioner Jameson explained that Arthur Young and Company was "recommended to us by a Mr. Catherwood. ... We asked them to come to Ottawa and discuss matters with us, and a representative of their firm came to Ottawa and discussed the subject and we engaged them." Canada, House of Commons, Special Committee on the Civil Service of Canada (Malcolm Committee), *Reports of the Committee, Journals of the House of Commons*. 14th Parliament, 2nd Session, vol. 60, January–July 1923 (Ottawa: King's Printer, 1923), Appendix 5.

155 A "typical list of clients" of the Industrial Engineering Department is provided in a memorandum prepared by Griffenhagen for Prime Minister Arthur Meighen in 1921: Edwin O. Griffenhagen, "Memorandum Regarding the Professional Record of Messrs. Arthur Young and Company and Griffenhagen and Associates, Ltd.," 23 August 1921 (Ottawa: National Archives of Canada, Arthur Meighen Papers, vol. 19), pp. 10725–32. Almost all of the

states and cities listed as clients in this memorandum retained Griffenhagen in 1919–20, after work for the Canadian government had begun.

156 The members of the staff who worked on the Canadian contract are listed in Canada, Civil Service Commission, "Response to Questions of Mr. Gavreau," Can. Sess. Pap. 10 George V (1920), no. 139 [unpublished].

157 Arthur Young and Company, *Civil Service Commission of Canada: Report on Office Organization and Procedure* (Ottawa, 1918) [unpublished].

158 Fred Telford, Resumé, (Washington, D.C.: Brookings Institution Archives, Bureau of Public Personnel Administration Files, Entry 179).

159 Arthur Young and Company, *Report of Transmission to Accompany the Classification of the Civil Service of Canada* (Ottawa: King's Printer, 1919), p. 76.

160 Canada, Civil Service Commission, *Report of the Commissioners, 1917–18*, Can. Sess. Pap. 9 George V (1919), no. 31. Compare to the quotation from Robert Catherwood on page 24.

161 Ibid., pp. 24 and 27.

162 Bill 136 was given first reading on 10 June 1919. The "Book of Classification" was released by the commission on June 17.

163 Arthur Young and Company, *Classification of the Civil Service of Canada* (Ottawa: King's Printer, 1919).

164 Canada, Civil Service Commission, *Information Respecting Promotions in the Civil Service* (Ottawa: King's Printer, 1921), p. 4.

165 Dawson, *Civil Service of Canada*, p. 95.

166 Griffenhagen was undoubtedly embarrassed by the delay in completing the report. He had originally told the government that his work would be done by December 1918, if not earlier. Canada, House of Commons, *Debates*. 13th Parliament, 1st Session, vol. 2, 10 May 1918 (Ottawa: King's Printer, 1918), p. 1902.

167 "The Classification," *Ottawa Journal*, 15 July 1919, p. 6.

168 "Answers Queries from Employees of Government," *Ottawa Journal*, 16 July 1919, p. 16.

169 Malcolm Committee, *Reports*, pp. 226 and 897–8.

170 Griffenhagen, "Principle and Technique of Preparing an Occupational Classification," *Public Personnel Studies*, p. 251.

171 "On Understanding Re-Classification," *The Ottawa Citizen*, 19 June 1919, p. 17.

172 Canada, House of Commons, *Debates*. 13th Parliament, 2nd Session, vol. 4, 24 June 1919 (Ottawa: King's Printer, 1919), p. 3927.

173 "Classification Is Approved By Meeting Of C.S. Employees," *Ottawa Journal*, 2 October 1919, p. 7.

174 "Vagaries of Classification," *Ottawa Journal*, 26 June 1919, p. 6.

175 "Postal Workers Are Not Satisfied," *Ottawa Journal*, 27 June 1919, p. 2.

176 "Civil Servant Criticizes Proposed Classification," *Ottawa Journal*, 30 September 1919, p. 15.

177 Dawson, *Civil Service of Canada*, p. 95.

178 "Silas Answers Questions For The Service," *Ottawa Journal*, 20 September 1919, p. 1.

179 Arthur Young and Company, *Report of Transmission*, p. 12; Griffenhagen, "Principle and Technique of Preparing an Occupational Classification," *Public Personnel Studies*, p. 244.

180 Arthur Young and Company, *Report of Transmission*, p. 11.

181 See Frank B. and Lillian M. Gilbreth, "The Three-Position Plan of Promotion," *Iron Age* 96 (1915), pp. 1057–9; and "The Three-Position Plan of Promotion," *Annals* 65 (1916), pp. 289–96.

182 "C.S. Complaints Are Blamed For Delayed Report," *Ottawa Journal*, 9 July 1919, p. 2.

183 Canada, Civil Service Commission, *Report of the Commissioners, 1918–19*, Can. Sess. Pap. 10 George V (1920), no. 32.

184 *Ottawa Journal*, 3 July 1919, p. 6.

185 "Civil Service Adopts Report on the Bonuses," *Ottawa Journal*, 4 July 1919, p. 16. Jacobs had been fired from the efficiency division of the Chicago Commission in 1915, shortly after the election of Mayor Thompson. He started his own consulting firm, which by 1919 had crafted reforms on the Chicago model for the City of Milwaukee and the State of New Jersey. See Joseph B. Kingsbury, "The Merit System in Chicago from 1915 to 1923," *Public Personnel Studies* 4:11 (November 1926), p. 307; William C. Beyer, "Classification and Standardization of Personal Service," *National Municipal Review* 6:6 (November 1917), p. 751; William C. Beyer, "Salary Standardization in the New Jersey State Government," *National Municipal Review* 7:3 (May 1918), p. 306.

186 "Postal Workers Are Not Satisfied," *Ottawa Journal*, 27 June 1919, p. 2; "New Civil Service Bill Denounced By Veterans," *Ottawa Journal*, 12 July 1919, p. 4.

187 See Samuel Chandler, Letter to the Editor, *Ottawa Journal*, 11 July 1919, p. 6.

188 "Bonus Statement Is Eagerly Awaited," *Ottawa Journal*, 4 July 1919, p. 4.

189 See Malcolm Committee, *Reports*, Exhibit F.

190 J.E. Hodgetts et al., *The Biography of an Institution: The Civil Service Commission of Canada, 1908–1967* (Montreal: McGill-Queen's University Press, 1972), p. 74.

191 Ottawa gossip said that the commission considered Griffenhagen's work to be "most unsatisfactory." William Roche was eventually prodded to write to the prime minister to deny that this was so – although he would not deny that "an individual member or members of the Commission or its staff may have so expressed themselves. ... Strained relations, to put it mildly, existed between my colleagues on the Commission and the employees of the Arthur Young Company." William Roche to Arthur Meighen, [letter] 26 August 1921 (Ottawa: National Archives of Canada, Arthur Meighen Papers, vol. 19), pp. 10715–17.

192 "Select Board To Deal With C.S. Appeals," *Ottawa Journal*, 13 August 1919, p. 7; "Will Adjust Claims With New Bureau," *Ottawa Journal*, 9 September 1919, p. 1.

193 "Board to Adjust C.S. Classification," *Ottawa Journal*, 8 August 1919, p. 5.

194 Malcolm Committee, *Reports*, pp. 227–8.

195 Ibid., pp. 761–2.

196 Ibid., p. 179.

197 See Canada, Dominion Bureau of Statistics, *Statement of Civil Service Personnel and Salaries in the Month of January 1912–1924* (Ottawa: King's Printer, 1924), Table C. The commission had also moved to new and much larger offices in the Hunter Building, at O'Connor and Queen streets.

198 Shortt to Warburton, [letter] 4 January 1918.

199 Adam Shortt to A.G. Doughty, [letter] 12 January 1918 (Ottawa: National Archives of Canada, Record Group 32, File of Dr. A. Shortt, vol. 366.

200 Adam Shortt to Sir George Foster, [letter] 30 March 1918 (Kingston: Queen's University Archives, Adam Shortt Papers, Correspondence File).

201 William Foran to Adam Shortt, [letter] 26 March 1918 (Kingston: Queen's University Archives, Adam Shortt Papers, Correspondence File).

202 Malcolm Committee, *Reports*, p. 733.

203 Ibid., p. 634.

204 Ibid., p. 629.

205 Ibid., p. 756.

206 Ibid., pp. 795–6.

207 Ibid., pp. 761–2.

208 *Ottawa Journal*, 24 October 1919, p. 1.

209 "House To Adopt C.S. Measure," *Ottawa Journal*, 6 October 1919, p. 1.

210 Sir George Perley to Sir George Foster, [letter] 19 April 1920 (Ottawa: National Archives of Canada, Record Group 32, vol. 410). For a variety of reasons, the High Commission's records of the troubles caused by the new classification plan are the most extensive available for any department.

211 Canada, House of Commons, *Debates*. 13th Parliament, 5th Session, vol. 3, 2 May 1921 (Ottawa: King's Printer, 1921), p. 2835.

212 *The Ottawa Citizen*, 6 May 1921, p. 3.

213 Ibid., 2 May 1921, p. 3.

214 Ibid., 9 May 1921, p. 11.

215 Sir Joseph Pope to W.L. Griffith, [letter] 8 June 1921, (Ottawa: National Archives of Canada, Sir Joseph Pope Papers, vol. 30, ser. no. 923); Malcolm Committee, *Reports*, p. 754.

216 Sir Joseph Pope, [diary] 30 June 1921 (Ottawa: National Archives of Canada, Sir Joseph Pope Papers, vol. 47); Canada, House of Commons, *Debates*. 14th Parliament, 2nd Session, vol. 1, 22 February 1923 (Ottawa: King's Printer, 1923), p. 564.

217 Pope, *Memoirs of a Public Servant*, p. 289.

218 Malcolm Committee, *Reports*, Appendix L, [emphasis in the original].

219 See Canada, Civil Service Commission, *Report of the Commissioners, 1918–19*, pp. 9–11; Arthur Young and Company, *Report of Transmission*, p. 21.

220 Shortt to Grant, [letter] 16 March 1923.

221 Malcolm Committee, *Reports*, p. 54.

222 See the quotation from Catherwood on page 28 of this book.

223 Malcolm Committee, *Reports*, p. xii.

224 "Offer $2,800 Salary For Chief Organizer," *Ottawa Journal*, 25 July 1919, p. 18.

225 Canada, Civil Service Commission, *Examination Papers, 1919*, Can. Sess. Pap. 10 George V (1920), no. 31, p. 158.

226 Canada, Civil Service Commission, Organization Branch, "Memorandum on Reorganization of Government Departments or Branches," 15 April 1924 (Ottawa: National Archives of Canada, Record Group 32, vol. 893, series H).

227 Griffenhagen himself was retained to complete some reorganizational work for the government. Because the commission declined to supervise this project, Griffenhagen reported instead to a committee of cabinet. Over one hundred reports and memoranda were presented to the subcommittee, but only a handful of reforms were adopted. Meanwhile, Griffenhagen's investigations caused intense disgruntlement within the civil service. The government cancelled its contract with Griffenhagen in February 1921. See Hodgetts et al., *Biography of an Institution*, pp. 75–90 and 100–103.

228 Ibid., p. 353.

229 Arthur Young and Company, *Report of Transmission*, p. 73.

230 See, for example, Foran to Shortt, [letter] 26 March 1918.

231 Canada, Civil Service Commission, *Information Respecting Technical Positions in the Civil Service of Canada* (Ottawa: King's Printer, 1921).

232 Arthur Young and Company, *Report of Transmission*, pp. 35–62.

233 Ibid., p. 65.

234 United States, Congressional Joint Commission on Reclassification of Salaries, *Report*, 66th Congress, 2nd Session, 1920, House of Representatives Document 686.

235 Canada, Civil Service Commission, *Report of the Commissioners, 1917–18*, p. 16.

236 Arthur Young and Company, *Report of Transmission*, pp. vi and 57; Congressional Joint Commission on Reclassification of Salaries, *Report*, p. 150.

237 Arthur Young and Company, *Report of Transmission*, pp. 78–9; *Debates*. 13th Parliament, 2nd Session, vol. 3, 12 May 1919, p. 2293.

238 New York Bureau of Municipal Research, "Standardization of Municipal Employments, Part II," *Municipal Research* 76 (August 1916), p. 45–83; Congressional Joint Commission on Reclassification of Salaries, *Report*, p. 149.

239 Canada, Civil Service Commission, "Response to Questions of Mr. Gavreau," [unpublished].

240 Arthur Young and Company, *Report of Transmission*, p. 72.

241 Ibid., p. 65.

242 Edwin O. Griffenhagen, "A Farewell Contribution from Griffenhagen and Associates," *The Civilian* (February 1921), pp. 70–1.

243 Griffenhagen, "Origin of the Modern Occupational Classification," *Public Personnel Studies*, p. 194.

244 Canada, Civil Service Commission, *Report of the Commissioners, 1917–18*, p. 24.

245 I am indebted to Professor J.E. Hodgetts for pointing this out to me.

246 Hodgetts et al., *Biography of an Institution*, p. 69.

247 Canada, Civil Service Commission, *Report of the Commissioners, 1918–19*, p. 12.

248 Meriam, "Uses of a Personnel Classification in the Public Service," *Annals*, p. 216. Lewis Meriam worked for Griffenhagen on the reclassification of the U.S. executive departments in 1920.

249 Malcolm Committee, *Reports*, p. 907.

250 *Debates*. 13th Parliament, 2nd Session, vol. 3, 28 May 1919, p. 2911.

251 Ibid., p. 2912.

252 *Ottawa Journal*, 30 September 1919, p. 15.

253 *Debates.* 13th Parliament, 2nd Session, vol. 4, 24 June 1919, p. 3927.

254 "Sir George Begins Work," *Ottawa Journal*, 30 September 1912, p. 1.

255 Quoted in Hodgetts et al., *Biography of an Institution*, p. 357.

256 "As an organization endeavouring to establish a base of support, the CSC laboured under the compulsion to explain the reason for its special role in making appointments, promotions, and in conducting classification work. ... By giving its procedure, in practice and in theory, the attributes of a machine which scientifically and remorselessly chose the one best candidate for any given job, the CSC could justify its special competence to perform these tasks" (Ibid., 356–7).

257 National Assembly of Civil Service Commissions, *Draft of a Civil Service Law* (Washington: National Assembly of Civil Service Commissions, 1916), p. 3.

258 National Municipal League, "National Municipal League Committees 1918–1919," *National Municipal Review* 7:6 (November 1918), p. 653.

259 See Adam Shortt, [diary], 2 December 1918 (Kingston: Queen's University Archives, Adam Shortt Papers, Box 11, File 11).

260 National Civil Service Reform League, *Proceedings of the Thirty-Eighth Annual Meeting* (New York: National Civil Service Reform League, 1919).

261 "Chicago Aldermen Visit The Capital," *Ottawa Journal*, 27 October 1919, p. 16.

262 National Civil Service Reform League, *Proceedings of the Thirty-Eighth Annual Meeting*, pp. 27 and 39.

263 Arthur Young and Company, *Report of Transmission*, p. 65.

264 Frank Davidson, *Management Consultants* (London: Nelson, 1972).

265 Laura Tatham, *The Efficiency Experts* (London: Business Publications, 1964), p. 11.

266 W.M. Greenfield, *Successful Management Consulting* (Englewood Cliffs, N.J.: Prentice-Hall, 1987), p. 38.

267 See also Peter L. Berger and T. Luckmann, *The Social Construction of Reality* (New York: Doubleday, 1966), p. 88.

268 See Guy Benveniste, *The Politics of Expertise* (Berkeley, Calif.: Glendessary Press, 1972), pp. 126–7.

269 See Theodore M. Becker and R.N. Stern, "Professionalism, Professionalization, and Bias in the Commercial Human Relations Consulting Operation," *Journal of Business* 46:2 (1973), pp. 240–1.

270 Luther Gulick, "Science, Values and Administration," in L. Gulick and L. Urwick, eds., *Papers on the Science of Administration* (New York: Institute of Public Administration, 1937).

271 Information on Griffenhagen's public sector work may be found in Griffenhagen, "Memorandum Regarding the Professional Record of Messrs. Arthur Young and Company and Griffenhagen and Associates, Ltd"; E.O. Griffenhagen, "Memorandum Respecting the Work of Griffenhagen and Associates, Ltd.," 26 March 1926 (Chicago: Chicago Historical Society Archives, William A. Dever Papers); William C. Beyer, *Personnel Administration in Philadelphia* (Philadelphia: Bureau of Municipal Research, 1937), p. 39; William E. Mosher

and J.D. Kingsley, *Public Personnel Administration* (New York: Harper and Brothers, 1936), p. 356.

272 Herbert D. Brown to Adam Shortt, [letter] 16 April 1919 (Kingston: Queen's University Archives, Adam Shortt Papers, Correspondence Files); Clinton Rogers Woodruff, "Classification and Salary Standardization in Philadelphia," *National Municipal Review* 9:7 (July 1920), p. 416; United States, Congressional Joint Commission on Reclassification of Salaries, *Report*; Griffenhagen, "Memorandum Respecting the Work of Griffenhagen and Associates, Ltd.," p. 2.

273 Sir Robert Borden to A.K. Maclean, [letter] 17 February 1931 (Ottawa: National Archives of Canada, Sir Robert Borden Papers, vol. 265), p. 148633.

274 Borden, *Problems of an Efficient Civil Service*, p. 18.

275 Robert C. Catherwood to Sir Robert Borden, [letter] 25 December 1930 (Ottawa: National Archives of Canada, Sir Robert Borden Papers, vol. 265), p. 148608.

276 Robert C. Catherwood to Sir Robert Borden, [letter] 28 November 1931 (Ottawa: National Archives of Canada, Sir Robert Borden Papers, vol. 265), p. 148855.

277 Robert C. Catherwood to Sir Robert Borden, [letter] 5 March 1931 (Ottawa: National Archives of Canada, Sir Robert Borden Papers, vol. 265), p. 148638.

278 Sir Robert Borden to Robert C. Catherwood, [letter] 14 March 1931 (Ottawa: National Archives of Canada, Sir Robert Borden Papers, vol. 265), p. 148639.

Bibliography

MANUSCRIPT COLLECTIONS

Unfortunately the records of the Civil Service Commission of Canada for this period have been largely destroyed or lost. Some remaining papers may be found in the National Archives of Canada, Record Group 32, volumes 893 and 1021. Personnel Files for William Foran and Adam Shortt may be found in Record Group 32, volumes 93 (for Foran) and 366 (for Shortt). The records of the Canadian High Commission in London also contain a significant amount of material relating to the reclassification: see Record Group 32, volume 410.

I have also drawn on the following collections:
Sir Robert Borden Papers. National Archives of Canada, Ottawa.
Louis Brownlow Papers. John F. Kennedy Library Archives, Boston, Mass.
Mayor William A. Dever Papers. Chicago Historical Society Archives.
Sir George Foster Papers. National Archives of Canada.
William Grant Papers. National Archives of Canada.
Arthur Meighen Papers. National Archives of Canada.
Sir Joseph Pope Papers. National Archives of Canada.
Adam Shortt Papers. Queen's University Archives, Kingston.
Papers of the Bureau of Public Personnel Administration. Brookings Institution Archives, Washington, D.C.
I regret that I was unable to find the papers of Edwin Griffenhagen or of his firm, Griffenhagen and Associates. The scholar who succeeds in discovering them will have found quite a prize.

PERIODICALS

National Municipal Review, 1910–1920.
The New York Times, February 1982.
The Ottawa Citizen, June–October 1919; May 1921.

Ottawa Journal, September 1912; June 1916; June–October 1919; January 1939.

BOOKS AND ARTICLES

Arthur Young and Company. *Civil Service Commission of Canada: Report on Office Organization and Procedure*. Ottawa, 1918 [unpublished].

—. *Classification of the Civil Service of Canada*. Ottawa: King's Printer, 1919.

—. *Report of Transmission to Accompany the Classification of the Civil Service of Canada*. Ottawa: King's Printer, 1919.

Atkinson, C.R. "Recent Graft Exposures and Prosecutions." *National Municipal Review* 1:4 (October 1912): 672–9.

Beard, Charles. "Chicago Treasurers to Face Charge." *National Municipal Review* 1:1 (1912): 157.

Becker, Theodore M., and R.N. Stern. "Professionalism, Professionalization, and Bias in the Commercial Human Relations Consulting Operation." *Journal of Business* 46:2 (1973): 230–57.

Benveniste, Guy. *The Politics of Expertise*. Berkeley: Glendessary Press, 1972.

Berger, Peter L., and T. Luckmann. *The Social Construction of Reality*. New York: Doubleday, 1966.

Beyer, William C. "Standardization of Salaries in American Cities." *National Municipal Review* 5:2 (April 1916): 266–72.

—. "Classification and Standardization of Personal Service." *National Municipal Review* 6:6 (November 1917): 751.

—. "Salary Standardization in the New Jersey State Government." *National Municipal Review* 7:3 (May 1918): 306–7.

—. *Personnel Administration in Philadelphia*. Philadelphia: Bureau of Municipal Research, 1937.

Bishop, Glen A., ed. *Chicago's Accomplishments and Leaders*. Chicago: Bishop Publishing, 1933.

Borden, Sir Robert. *Problems of An Efficient Civil Service*. Ottawa: King's Printer, 1931.

—. *Memoirs*. New York: Macmillan, 1938.

Brownell, Blaine, and W. Stickle., eds. *Bosses and Reformers: Urban Politics in America, 1880–1920*. Boston: Houghton Mifflin, 1973.

Campbell, J.E. "Powers Which Should Be Exercised By A Civil Service Commission." In National Assembly of Civil Service Commissions, *Proceedings of the Seventh Annual Meeting*. New York: Chief Publishing Company, 1914.

Canada. Civil Service Commission. *First Annual Report*. Can. Sess. Pap. 9–10 Edward VII (1910), no. 31.

—. —. *Examination Papers, 1913–14*. Can. Sess. Pap. 5 George V (1915), no. 31.

—. —. *Report of the Commissioners, 1914–15*. Can. Sess. Pap. 6 George V (1916), no. 31.

—. —. *Report of the Commissioners, 1917–1918*. Can. Sess. Pap. 9 George V (1919), no. 31.

—. —. *Report of the Commissioners, 1918–1919*. Can. Sess. Pap. 10 George V (1920),

no. 32.
—. —. *Examination Papers, 1919*. Can. Sess. Pap. 10 George V (1920), no. 31.
—. —. "Response to Questions of Mr. Gavreau." Can. Sess. Pap. 10 George V (1920), no. 139 [unpublished].
—. —. *Information Respecting Technical Positions in the Civil Service of Canada*. Ottawa: King's Printer, 1921.
—. —. *Information Respecting Promotions in the Civil Service*. Ottawa: King's Printer, 1921.
—. Dominion Bureau of Statistics. *Statement of Civil Service Personnel and Salaries in the Month of January, 1912–1924*. Ottawa: King's Printer, 1924.
—. House of Commons. *Debates*. 13th Parliament, 1st Session, vols. 1–2. 19 March – 10 May 1918. Ottawa: King's Printer, 1918.
—. —. —. 13th Parliament, 2nd Session, vols. 3–4. 12 May – 24 June 1919. Ottawa: King's Printer, 1919.
—. —. —. 13th Parliament, 5th Session, vol. 3. 2 May 1921. Ottawa: King's Printer, 1921.
—. —. —. 14th Parliament, 2nd Session, vol. 1. 22 February 1923. Ottawa: King's Printer, 1923.
—. —. —. 34th Parliament, 3rd Session, vols. 5–10. 10 February–23 June 1992. Ottawa: Supply and Services Canada, 1992.
—. —. Legislative Committee on Bill C-26. *Minutes and Proceedings*. 34th Parliament, 3rd Session, nos. 1–13. 9 March–2 April 1992. Ottawa: Supply and Services Canada, 1992.
—. —. Special Committee on the Civil Service of Canada (Malcolm Committee). *Reports of the Committee. Journals of the House of Commons*. 14th Parliament, 2nd session, vol. 60. January–July 1923. Ottawa: King's Printer, 1923.
—. Public Service 2000. *The Renewal of the Public Service of Canada: Synopsis*. Ottawa: Supply and Services Canada, 1990.
—. —. *Report of the Task Force on Staffing*. Ottawa: Privy Council Office, 1990.
—. Royal Commission on Administrative Classifications in the Public Service (Gordon Commission). *Report of the Royal Commission*. Ottawa: King's Printer, 1946.
—. Royal Commission on Civil Service (McInnes Commission). *Report of the Commissioners*. Can. Sess. Pap. 44 Victoria (1881), no. 113.
—. Royal Commission on Civil Service (Hague Commission). *Report of the Commissioners*. Can. Sess. Pap. 55 Victoria (1892), no. 16c.
—. Royal Commission on Civil Service (Courtney Commission). *Report of the Commissioners*. Can. Sess. Pap. 7 Edward VII (1907), no. 29a.
—. Royal Commission on Financial Management and Accountability (Lambert Commission). *Final Report*. Ottawa: Supply and Services Canada, 1979.
—. Royal Commission on Government Organization (Glassco Commission). *Management of the Public Service*. Ottawa: Queen's Printer, 1962.
—. Royal Commission on Technical and Professional Services (Beatty Commission). *Report*. Ottawa: King's Printer, 1930.
—. Statutes of Canada. Civil Service Amendment Act, 1908. 7–8 Edward VII, c. 15.

—. —. Civil Service Act, 1918. 8–9 George V, c. 12.

—. —. Civil Service Amendment Act. 10 George V, c. 10

Catherwood, Robert C. "Efficiency in the Public Service of Chicago." In National Civil Service Reform League, *Proceedings of the Twenty-Eighth Annual Meeting*. Chicago: National Civil Service Reform League, 1909.

—. "The Development of Efficiency in the Civil Service." In National Civil Service Reform League, *Proceedings of the Twenty-Ninth Annual Meeting*. Chicago: National Civil Service Reform League, 1910.

—. "The Investigation of Chicago's Police." *National Municipal Review* 1:2 (April 1912): 289–91.

—. "Widening of the Area of the Functions of Civil Service Commissions." In National Assembly of Civil Service Commissions, *Proceedings of the Sixth Annual Meeting*. New York: Chief Publishing Company, 1913.

—. "Essential Principles of a Model Civil Service Law for States, Counties, and Cities." In National Assembly of Civil Service Commissions, *Proceedings of the Seventh Annual Meeting*. New York: Chief Publishing Company, 1914.

—. "A Model Civil Service Law." In National Assembly of Civil Service Commissions, *Proceedings of the Eighth Annual Meeting*. New York: Chief Publishing Company, 1915.

—. "The Future of the Merit System." In National Assembly of Civil Service Commissions, *Proceedings of the Eighth Annual Meeting*. New York: Chief Publishing Company, 1915.

Chicago. Civil Service Commission. *Fourteenth Annual Report*. Chicago: Civil Service Commission, 1909.

—. —. *Seventeenth Annual Report*. Chicago: Civil Service Commission, 1912.

—. —. *Eighteenth Annual Report*. Chicago: Civil Service Commission, 1913.

Cole, Taylor. *The Canadian Bureaucracy*. Durham, N.C.: Duke University Press, 1949.

Dauchy, Samuel. "Report on the Illinois Civil Service Commissions." In National Civil Service Reform League, *Proceedings of the Thirty-Second Annual Meeting*. Chicago: National Civil Service Reform League, 1913.

Davidson, Frank. *Management Consultants*. London: Nelson, 1972.

Dawson, R. McGregor. *The Civil Service of Canada*. London: Humphrey Milford, 1929.

—. "The Canadian Civil Service." *Canadian Journal of Economics and Political Science* 2:3 (August 1936): 288–300.

Faught, Albert S. "A Review of the Civil Service Laws of the United States." *National Municipal Review* 3:2 (April 1914): 316–26.

—. "Mr. Catherwood's Draft of a Model Civil Service Law." *National Municipal Review* 3:2 (April 1914): 377–9.

Flanagan, Maureen. *Charter Reform in Chicago*. Carbondale, Ill.: Southern Illinois University Press, 1987.

—. "Fred A. Busse: A Silent Mayor in Turbulent Times." In Paul Green and M.G. Holli, eds. *The Mayors: The Chicago Political Tradition*. Carbondale, Ill.: Southern Illinois University Press, 1987.

Foran, William. "The Civil Service Law in Canada." In National Assembly of Civil

Service Commissions, *Proceedings of the Eighth Annual Meeting*. New York: Chief Publishing Company, 1915.

Foulke, W.D. *Fighting the Spoilsman*. New York: G.P. Putnam's Sons, 1919.

Gilbreth, Frank B. *Primer of Scientific Management*. New York: Van Nostrand Company, 1912.

—, and L.M. Gilbreth. "The Three-Position Plan of Promotion." *Iron Age* 96 (1915): 1057–9.

—, and L.M. Gilbreth. "The Three-Position Plan of Promotion." *Annals* 65 (1916): 289–96.

Grant, William L. "The Civil Service of Canada." *The University of Toronto Quarterly* 3:4 (July 1934): 428–38.

Greenfield, W.M. *Successful Management Consulting*. Englewood Cliffs, N.J.: Prentice-Hall, 1987.

Griffenhagen, Edwin O. "A Farewell Contribution from Griffenhagen and Associates." *The Civilian* (February 1921): 70–1.

—. "Memorandum Regarding the Professional Record of Messrs. Arthur Young and Company and Griffenhagen and Associates, Ltd." 23 August 1921. Ottawa: National Archives of Canada. Arthur Meighen Papers, vol. 19.

—. "The Origin of the Modern Occupational Classification in Personnel Administration." *Public Personnel Studies* 2:6 (September 1924): 184–94.

—. "The Principle and Technique of Preparing an Occupational Classification of Positions in the Public Service." *Public Personnel Studies* 2:8 (November 1924): 240–53.

Gulick, Luther. "Science, Values and Administration." In L. Gulick and L. Urwick, eds. *Papers on the Science of Administration*. New York: Institute of Public Administration, 1937.

Haydon, Andrew. "Adam Shortt." *Queen's Quarterly* 38 (Autumn 1931): 609–23.

Hays, Samuel. "The Politics of Reform in Municipal Government in the Progressive Era." In Blaine Brownell and W. Stickle, eds. *Bosses and Reformers: Urban Politics in America, 1880–1920*. Boston: Houghton Mifflin Company, 1973.

Hodgetts, J.E., et al. *The Biography of an Institution: The Civil Service Commission of Canada, 1908–1967*. Montreal: McGill-Queen's University Press, 1972.

Hofstadter, Richard. *The Age of Reform*. New York: Vintage Books, 1955.

Hood, Christopher, and Michael Jackson. *Administrative Argument*. London: Gower, 1991.

—. "Keys for Locks in Administrative Argument." *Administration and Society* 25:4 (February 1994): 467–88.

Hoogenboom, Ari. *Outlawing the Spoils*. Urbana, Ill.: University of Illinois Press, 1961.

Hopkins, J.C. *Canadian Annual Review, 1907*. Toronto: Annual Review Publishing Company, 1908.

—. *Canadian Annual Review, 1917*. Toronto: Annual Review Publishing Company, 1918.

Jacobs, J. Louis. "Standardizing Efficiency in Chicago." In National Assembly of Civil Service Commissions, *Proceedings of the Sixth Annual Meeting*. New York: Chief Publishing Company, 1913.

—. *Review of Movement for Standardization of Public Employments.* Chicago: J.L. Jacobs Company, 1916.

Kingsbury, Joseph B. "The Merit System in Chicago from 1895 to 1915, Part 4." *Public Personnel Studies* 4:6 (June 1926): 178–84.

—. "The Merit System in Chicago from 1915 to 1923." *Public Personnel Studies.* 4:11 (November 1926): 306–18.

Lewis, John. "The Laurier Regime, 1896–1911." In A. Shortt and A.G. Doughty, eds. *Canada and Its Provinces,* vol. 6. Toronto: Glasgow, Brook, and Company, 1914.

Lindberg, Richard. *To Serve and Collect: Chicago Politics and Police Corruption.* New York: Praeger, 1991.

Lower, Elton. "Movement for Efficiency." In National Assembly of Civil Service Commissions, *Proceedings of the Fourth Meeting.* New York: Chief Publishing Company, 1911.

Mallory, James R. *The Structure of Canadian Government.* Toronto: Macmillan, 1970.

March, James G., and Johan P. Olsen. *Rediscovering Institutions.* New York: Free Press, 1989.

Marquis, Albert N., ed. *Who's Who in America, 1926–27.* Chicago: A.N. Marquis Company, 1927.

McCarthy, Michael P. "Businessmen and Professionals in Municipal Reform: The Chicago Experience, 1887–1920." Ph.D. diss., Northwestern University, 1970.

Meriam, Lewis. "The Uses of a Personnel Classification in the Public Service." *Annals* 113 (1924): 215–19.

Merriam, Charles E. "Investigations as a Means of Securing Administrative Efficiency." *Annals* 41 (1912): 281–303.

—. *Chicago.* New York: Macmillan, 1929.

Miles, James. "Municipal Efficiency: What Is It?" In National Assembly of Civil Service Commissions. *Proceedings of the Fifth Annual Meeting.* New York: Chief Publishing Company, 1912.

Mosher, William E., and J.D. Kingsley. *Public Personnel Administration.* New York: Harper and Brothers, 1936.

Murray, Sir George. *Report on the Organization of the Public Service of Canada.* Can. Sess. Pap. 3 George V (1912), no. 57a.

National Assembly of Civil Service Commissions. *Proceedings of the Fourth Annual Meeting.* New York: Chief Publishing Company, 1911.

—. *Proceedings of the Fifth Annual Meeting.* New York: Chief Publishing Company, 1912.

—. *Proceedings of the Eighth Annual Meeting.* New York: Chief Publishing Company, 1915.

—. *Proceedings of the Ninth Annual Meeting.* Ottawa: King's Printer, 1916.

—. *Draft of a Standard Civil Service Law.* Washington: National Assembly of Civil Service Commissions, 1916.

National Civil Service Reform League. *Proceedings of the Thirty-Eighth Annual Meeting.* New York: National Civil Service Reform League, 1919.

National Municipal League. "National Municipal League Committees 1918–1919." *National Municipal Review* 7:6 (November 1918): 652–5.

New York Bureau of Municipal Research. "Standardization of Public Employments, Part I." *Municipal Research* 67 (November 1915): 1–44.
—. "Standardization of Municipal Employments, Part II." *Municipal Research* 76 (August 1916): 45–83.
Parliamentary Press Gallery. *Canadian Parliamentary Guide*, 1918. Ottawa: Mortimer Publishing, 1918.
Patton, Clifford W. *The Battle for Municipal Reform.* College Park, Md.: McGrath Publishing Company, 1940.
Pope, Sir Joseph. "The Federal Government." In A. Shortt and A.G. Doughty, eds. *Canada and Its Provinces*, vol. 6. Toronto: Glasgow, Brooks, and Company, 1914.
—. *Memoirs of a Public Servant.* Toronto: Oxford University Press, 1960.
Rex, Frederick. "Analysis of Measures Relating to Municipal Administration and Legislation Submitted to Popular Vote at the November Election." *National Muncipal Review* 6:3 (May 1917): 387–94.
Roberts, Alasdair. "The Rhetorical Problems of the Management Expert." Ph.D. diss., Harvard University, 1994.
—. "Demonstrating Neutrality: The Rockefeller Philanthropies and the Evolution of Public Administration, 1927–1936." *Public Administration Review* 54:3 (May/June 1994): 221–8.
—. "'Civic Discovery' as a Rhetorical Strategy." *Journal of Policy Analysis and Management* 14:2 (Spring 1995): 291–307.
—. "The Brownlow–Brookings Feud: The Politics of Dissent Within the Academic Community." 311–40. *Journal of Policy History* 7:3 (Summer 1995).
—. "Why the Brownlow Committee Failed: Neutrality and Partisanship in the Early Years of Public Administration." forthcoming in *Administration and Society.*
Spencer, Nelson. "New York City's Civil Service." *National Municipal Review* 5:1 (January 1916): 47–55.
Sutherland, Douglas. *Fifty Years on the Civic Front.* Chicago: Civic Federation, 1943.
Tatham, Laura. *The Efficiency Experts.* London: Business Publications, 1964.
Teaford, Jon C. *The Twentieth-Century American City.* 2nd edition. Baltimore: Johns Hopkins University Press, 1993.
United Kingdom. Royal Commission on the Civil Service (Macdonnell Commission). *Fourth Report.* Parliamentary Papers, 1914. Volume XVI. Cd. 7338.
United States. Congressional Joint Commission on Reclassification of Salaries. *Report.* 66th Congress, 2nd Session. 1920. House of Representatives Document 686.
Watkins, T.H. *Righteous Pilgrim: The Life and Times of Harold L. Ickes.* New York: Henry Holt and Company, 1990.
Weinstein, James. *The Corporate Ideal in the Liberal State.* Boston: Beacon Press, 1968.
Wendt, Lloyd, and H. Kogan. *Lords of the Levee.* Indianapolis, Ind.: Bobbs-Merrill Company, 1943.
—. *Big Bill of Chicago.* Indianapolis, Ind.: Bobbs-Merrill Company, 1953.
—. *Bosses in Lusty Chicago.* Bloomington, Ind.: Indiana University Press, 1974.
Wiebe, Robert. *Businessmen and Reform: A Study of the Progressive Movement.* Cambridge: Harvard University Press, 1962.

Woodruff, Clinton Rogers. "Other Attacks on the Civil Service." *National Municipal Review* 5:2 (April 1916): 379.

—. "Classification and Salary Standardization in Philadelphia." *National Municipal Review* 9:7 (July 1920): 413–16.